THE SPARK:
TIMES BEHIND ME

From Kwame Nkrumah to Hilla Limann

Georgina and all my children, brothers
and sister who always stand by me;

My son Peter, nephew Kwabena together with
Mark, Uncle Laud and Krobo Edusei who died
where
I could not see them buried.
May they rest in peace.

Joe, Baby and Baaba
who understand me

THE SPARK:
TIMES BEHIND ME

From Kwame Nkrumah
to Hilla Limann

KOFI BATSA

REX COLLINGS
LONDON
1985

ACKNOWLEDGEMENTS

I wish to express my appreciation for the generous assistance of many friends of mine who would prefer not to be publicly thanked.

For advice, support and ideas, I owe much to my wife, Georgina; and to Christine Blane I express my thanks for her tireless typing of the complicated manuscripts.

I wish to thank all those who helped me out of Ghana after the 31 December 1981 coup. I am sure without their assistance, protection and hospitality, I should not have lived to tell my story.

The mistakes are my own and I shall be grateful to any reader who points them out, however angrily, so that they can be put right in subsequent reprints.

First printed in Great Britain by Rex Collings Ltd.
6 Paddington Street, London W1

Basta, Kofi
  The spark.
  1. Ghana—Politics and government—To 1957
  2. Ghana—Politics and government—1957-1979
  3. Ghana—Politics and government—1979-
  966.7'03   DT510.62

ISBN 0-86036-204-3

CONTENTS

INTRODUCTION

It was a cold, cloudy, windy day in London. I was waiting gloomily at my flat for the Ghanaian friend to bring me the news that I hoped he would not bring.

When the BBC had rung me the day before to say that I was a wanted man in Ghana, my own country, I said that I had no comment to make, and that I would not believe the story until I had seen it in writing. Now, when my friend produced a copy of the paper that I used to be connected with and had been a director of for so many years, *The Daily Graphic*, I saw on the front page that it was true. The headline read:

BATSA, 2 OTHERS WANTED PERSONS

Three persons including the former Head of Military Intelligence, Col. Annor Odjidja, have been declared wanted people.

"A press statement issued in Accra yesterday and signed by Mr Ato Austin, PNDC Secretary for Information, named the other two as Mr Kofi Batsa Publicity Director of the dissolved Peoples National Party (PNP) and Mr Francis Poku formerly of the Special Branch. The statement said that in spite of repeated statements asking them to report either to the Police or Military Authorities, they had failed to do so. These persons, it stressed, have committed grievous offences against the people and the nation for which they have to answer. The statement, therefore, asked the people to co-operate with the police and military authorities to effect the arrest of the three men."

So it was true. Perhaps as an old journalist I am too fond of the printed word. Perhaps it was because it was a newspaper I knew very well but now I really did believe that I was a wanted man, though I could not understand how it could be said that I had committed 'grievous offences' against the people and the nation. I am a Ghanaian: for fifty-three years I had been one. And in those years I had been active in public and in private life, in ways that I had no need to be ashamed of and often to be proud of. Indeed , when I looked back there was a lot to be remembered with pleasure, and a lot with pride . . .

CHAPTER ONE
A LOOK BACK

I was born on 8 January 1931. I come from Piengwah in the Manya Krobo Division of Eastern Ghana. I was the fourth son of my father and so, as is traditional, was called Narh meaning '4'. I was also given the biblical names of 'Seth' and 'Samuel'.

My father was a school teacher in the local Presbyterian school, and so we were not rich, but we grew up, my brothers, my sister and I, a disciplined and happy household. My parents in fact had twelve children in all, but as was common in those days, the survivors only totalled six boys and one girl.

Krobo is in the Eastern Highlands of Ghana and we of the Manya Krobo think of ourselves as proud and determined people. There were two particular factors which were always felt to be of particular significance in our family, and which gave us still greater confidence and self-respect, in what was after all not a very wealthy or powerful situation. The first was that the people of Piengwah were thought of as those whose particular virtues of courage and whose warlike characteristics gave them the duty of being the protectors, in effect, of the whole of the area known as Manya Krobo; the word Piengwah itself means 'a big fence for protection'. The second was more directed to my family, and was that we were related to 'the Stool', which is the chieftaincy of the area. This connection with the leaders of the community gave a greater status and feeling of local pride to us all and led to the regular involvement of my father and other members of the family in the affairs of the district.

Our family household, wherever it was, was always attached to a school and to a church, or a mission. Education and religion were therefore the prevailing topics at home and must therefore have influenced us all in ways that are too great to be measured. There are, however, two habits or characteristics which I am conscious of, and which derive from the religious discipline of those days. The first is my love of singing, and particularly of singing hymns. I will sing hymns to myself, when I

am driving, when I am with my family, in fact wherever I am
and the familiar comfort of words and tunes remains.

'Lord, it belongs not to my care
Whether I die or live;
To love and serve thee is my share,
And this Thy Grace must give.'

That is one of my favourites, but while I have the chance I cannot resist writing down the best of all:

'God is working his purpose out as year succeeds to year,
Nearer and nearer draws the time, the time that shall surely be,
When the earth shall be filled with the Glory of God as the waters
    cover the sea.'

The other remaining habit is a straightforward reaction
against the discipline and church-going of childhood Sundays.
The relief, when I was a boy, when Monday came and normal
activities resumed, was enormous, and to this day I still find,
instinctively, that Monday morning provides a bracing and
invigorating challenge – the finest time of the week!

I am very proud, as we all are in my family, of the family
relationship to the chieftaincy, 'The Stool' as we call it. It was
in fact my great grand-uncle Sir Emmanuel Mate Kole I, who
was among the first chiefs in the whole of Africa to be knighted.
He was an educated man, a teacher like members of the family
since, and trained by the Basle Mission. I think that the knight-
hood was given to him in recognition of the dignity conferred by
a proper education. Anyway, it is in the family records that the
Prince of Wales himself gave my great-uncle the accolade in
Manya Krobo, when he visited Africa on a tour in 1924. The
present paramount chief is a cousin of my father, and like his
predecessors a highly respected man.

My father was brought up by the Presbyterians, in the same
tradition as my great-uncle and he became a teacher in the days
when one schoolmaster was responsible for the whole school,
and himself taught all subjects and controlled all six classes in
the school house.

My father was trained like all the other Presbyterian teachers
at the training college in Akropong and at the seminary at
Abetifi-Kwahu. It was the practice of the Basle missionaries to

train the local teachers to speak several languages of the country so that they could be posted from one school to the other. Thus my father could speak Krobo, our own language, Twi, and Ga, and I grew up with a smattering of all these languages. The teachers were therefore posted to any part of the country and their families followed them. This was, as can be imagined, not very good for a child's education and I had the general recollection from my primary school days of being moved from one school to another, from one half-mastered language to another, and from one set of friends to another.

My real education began when I was sent to the Bana Hill Presbyterian Senior School, which was famous in those days as being the school with the toughest discipline, both educationally and in a physical and social sense, in the whole country. Maybe it was the combination of the British public school tradition and Germanic discipline, but the system in my day at Bana Hill produced some remarkable results, both in and out of the classroom.

I always say that my life really began at Bana Hill and, quite apart from the work and the discipline, there was one particular incident which leads me to say this. The dormitories at Bana Hill for the Senior School pupils who were boarding, were grouped round a courtyard. In the middle of the courtyard there was placed every evening a large aluminium pot, and this served as the night-time lavatory for all boys in the dormitories. Any boy who wanted to urinate at any time of the night had to go to this pot for that purpose. Naturally in the morning this large pot had to be emptied and it was the duty of the younger boys to do this – in fact this was the task for the boys in the lowest form in the Senior School and a roster for this was made. I emptied the great pot once, and resolved that I would never do it again. I was very small and I could not even lift the pot so I had to use my own bucket to empty it. The whole affair was not only extremely unpleasant, but unhygenic as well as being unnecessary.

I had two weeks before my turn would come round again, so I consulted my friends. Because I was in the lowest form, and was indeed at that time the youngest in the school, I had not yet made many friends amongst the bigger boys, and my closest friends were in the Primary School, which was not far from our compound; they were in fact both cousins of mine, one was, in addition, the son of the headmaster, and his name was Teye Konotey-Ahulu. My other good friend, who grew up to be Colonel Lawrence Kodjiku, was another of my aunt's sons. Although I was the only one of the three who was directly affected by the problem of the giant pot, we all agreed that we would destroy it. So, one night soon after dark we took a machete and made a hole in the bottom of the pot, leaving it in its accustomed place in the middle of the yard. In the morning, as expected, the yard exuded a foul stench from the contents which had been spread over the ground.

The Headmaster, the Rev. Konotey-Ahulu, was of course extremely angry. He rightly suspected that the culprits must come from the bottom class, those who were responsible for emptying the pot. He lined us all up, including those in the classes close to us and who were suspected of being our friends. Forty-six pupils were lined up in the school compound when the Headmaster emerged from his office, walked towards us, came straight to me and said: 'I know you and your family, you cannot possibly have been involved in this affair. You can leave.' He then asked for confessions from the remaining forty-five and, when nobody confessed – as no one knew anything about the incident apart from myself and my two cousins in the other school – everyone received six strokes of the cane. I felt a little bad about being the only one, and the guilty one at that, to escape punishment, but I felt a great deal happier that the school could not afford to replace the aluminium pot, and so the practice of forcing the junior boys to empty it, ceased. I had the determination, even then, to fight for what I thought was right – and I had a lot of good fortune.

Ten years later the Rev. Konotey-Ahulu came to stay with me when I was teaching in Takoradi, and I confessed to him. He was astonished that the guilty ones included myself, and one of his own sons and, at that distance of time, roared with laughter. He told me later on that he had even used the story in his sermons.

Although this story remained secret, my general attitude did not – and neither did all schoolmasters take such a relaxed and cheerful attitude as the Rev. Konotey-Ahulu. Because, after the incident of the giant pot, I became the leader of the pupils in any argument which began about students' rights or discipline or privileges, and this continued in all of the schools that I found myself at. At Akro School, for example, I remember there was a Headmaster who was a very harsh disciplinarian. He had a great love of the cane and would use it freely on his pupils, often as a substitute for discussion, or for learning. As on other occasions I organized the class and I went to the bush and cut pieces of cane for the other pupils, to use if he attempted to beat us again. A 'black-leg' in the class told the master what was happening. He came to us the next day without a cane. He explained that he had only used the cane to 'train' us, if we objected to the use of the cane he would refrain from giving it to us, making the official quotation: 'The cane is for the back of the fool'. That was the end of the matter. Some years later I wanted to apply to the British Council for a Scholarship and I wrote to this Headmaster asking him to support me. He refused, expressing great surprise that I would think he would do any such thing. Years later, again, when I was Chairman of a Government Selection Committee, he applied for the post of Cultural Attaché in a Ghanaian Embassy. He was much the worst of the candidates, and did not get the job; but was loud in his accusations that it was my resentment for him that had caused him to fail.

This was the 1940s, years of colonial rule, and to struggle against authority of all kinds was the strongest instinct for many of us youngsters. And so, in taking the lead in many student arguments and strikes, I was expressing the mood of the times. But at the same time when I drew up petitions, had leaflets printed, or organized protests, I was also expressing the spirit of Piengwah, and my own character, my own fighting spirit.

Despite all this activity outside the classroom, I was quite a good student, and I took my courses seriously. Coming from my father's teaching background I could not do otherwise than work hard, and I read my way through his library when I was very young; the regular phrase of his that I still remember is 'Those books are too big for you'. I had taken to reading and I remember to this day, for example, a story called 'The vision of Mirza' from *The Royal Prince Reader*. But most of what I read, too old for me as it often was, led me to thoughts of things to fight for, and injustices which must be put right. My life was not entirely composed of pinning announcements on notice boards and signing petitions, but these were for me by far the most important activities, and even classwork was subordinate to this.

The story of how I became involved in communist activities brings together education, politics and the spirit of those times. By 1947 when Kwame Nkrumah returned to Accra from London, and politics in the Gold Coast came alive, I was myself nearly 18 and was at school in Accra. The atmosphere was stimulating as our new leaders and heroes told us of the evils of colonialism and how the white man was exploiting us and our country, and must soon leave. The leaders of political activity and of the United Gold Coast Convention were known as the Big Six – Dr J B Danquah, Edward Akuffo Addo, Ako Adjei, E O Obetsebi-Lamptey, William Ofori Atta and Kwame Nkrumah – but it was Nkrumah who was my hero from the start. Then, after the 1948 riots at 'The Christiansborg Crossroads', and the deaths that followed, the activities of the Watson Commission of Inquiry confirmed Nkrumah as the leader who really counted. The British press had always attempted to paint a picture of Nkrumah as a dangerous and militant communist revolutionary. The British lawyers taking part in the trial after the riots went out of their way to associate the overwhelmingly exciting atmosphere of nationalism and patriotism with communism – and in this way I became associated with communism; the association was made for me by the British press and by the British colonial Government. If my hero Kwame Nkrumah was responsible for importing communism into the Gold Coast, then communism, I thought, must be a good thing.

My favourite newspaper at that time was the Accra *Evening News*, I used to go down to the *Evening News* offices whenever I could, after school, and do any odd jobs that anyone would give me. I was always in the company of James Markham who was working on the paper. One day I happened to see lying on a table in the *Evening News* offices a leaflet from the Communist Party of Great Britain. Attracted by the heading, I read the leaflet right down to the coupon at the end which said 'If you want to join the Young Communist League of Great Britain –

return this coupon off to us'. Fired with patriotic enthusiasm, I sent the coupon off and soon received a letter from Britain assuring me that I would receive the Party literature and pamphlets, and saying that when I came to England I could be enrolled into the Party.

This Party literature was kept with great pride by my bed at my current school, The Washington Carver Institute which was established and run by the American Episcopal Church. It was not long before the Headmaster, Dr Ralph Shoneyeh Wright, found these dangerous-looking papers by my bed on one of his tours of inspection. In no time at all, the whole school was assembled, and Dr Wright embarked on a talk, which lasted nearly four hours, on the dangers of communism and the horror that there was in our midst a pupil who had 'joined the Communist Party'. Out of this great tirade, one which left a deep mark on me, the phrase that I still recall is 'You know what a communist is? He is the man who, if you talk to him, you wake up dead'.

Surprisingly, I did not leave the Washington Carver Institute after this traumatic event. I stayed on until the end of the academic year when I was going to leave anyway. This I think was because the Principal was slightly afraid of me, as I was an active student leader and I had backing in a formal as well as an informal way. He drew the line however at my being elected a prefect of the biggest house in the school; and although he had been praising the development of democracy in the school, he cancelled the election! So my last year at school, ended on an equivocal note, but I still remember the words written up over the entrance, 'Enter and learn. Go out and serve'. And the school motto is one which I firmly believed in then, and do now: *Non scholas sed vitae discimus* – We learn not for school but for life.

My closest friend at this time was Dr Ignatius Amuh, who later became a distinguished scientist in the field of atomic physics. Like me he was the son of poor parents and like me he was therefore at the school on a scholarship. (I had been a scholarship boy at most of my schools and indeed if I had not had scholarships, I would probably not have been at most of the schools I attended). Perhaps because he was also a poor boy, Amuh became my confidant. He joined me in writing up the articles and even before we left school we began writing regularly for the *Evening News*, articles on politics and the student movement – an activity in which we were later joined by another students, R S Awuku Appiah Nuamah, and Vincent Oware, hard working students. I broke down for three days when Dr Amuh died four years ago.

One of the leaders of the youth of the Convention People's Party at this time was Saki Scheck, and it was Saki Scheck who, together with Kofi Baako, became the main influences on my political development. Saki Scheck, who was Nkrumah's first private secretary, was a remarkably clear-headed man and a very precise, almost cold-blooded, political thinker. He was extremely clever and extremely ambitious, and while not necessarily an attractive character, he was a very able student of politics. Kofi Baako on the other hand, passionate and impulsive, would always rather act than consider, and could not have been a greater contrast. Between them, these two led the Youth of the CPP and it was a great pity, in my view, for the Party that Saki Scheck left so early in the movement and joined the Opposition. But it was these two who took me and my friends to see Kwame Nkrumah. When I left secondary school, in 1948, I had a confrontation with my father which involved some of the different strands in my life. I had known that my father wanted at least one of his sons to become a priest, but it was only when I went to see him after leaving school, that he said he wished me to be the one to join the Church, and go to the seminary at Trinity College, Kumasi. Now, as I have said, my involvement in politics, never mind Communism, would never have become so pronounced if I had not been away from home at a boarding school. At this stage, my father had no idea of my feelings. I did not tell him. I went back to Accra and wrote a long article in a paper that had just started to appear – *The Sunday Mirror* – and in it I said, and I can still quote this from memory, 'Men want to know the Church not as a doctrinal system but as a system of life and thought and whether what the Church is teaching is practicable in the kind of world in which we live'.

My father read the article and was furious; he would not speak to me for a year. But the question of my joining the Church never arose again. He withdrew my name from the Seminary – and sent a minister, the Rev. A C T Apo, to talk to me to try and discover 'why I let him down'.

Some time later, incidentally, when I was at home with my father, he was called on by Rev. Apo, my old Headmaster from Bana Hill, the Rev. Konotey-Ahulu, and Mr R P Djabanor. I went out to get some drinks for them and came back to find them gossiping and grumbling about the Church hierarchy and the individuals in it who were playing politics, or causing them trouble, or doing things they disapproved of. I told Rev. Apo later: 'And this is the organization you wanted me to join? I think it is just as well that I did not'. By then, however, they were not as much interested it seemed in my doctrinal lapse, but in the fact that I had overheard too much clerical gossip!

In a sense I reacted against the proposal that I should go into the Church in the same way that I reacted to a childhood of regimented Sundays, with relief, and by embracing the new freedom – the freedom of Monday, or the freedom of making up my own mind. I have come to my own religion in my own way since then and it is a great comfort to me. I pray, and think my prayers are heard. And the music of the Church is an additional pleasure; I was a chorister at all the schools, in those disciplined school days, and I still sing whenever I can, my love for it having come I think, from my mother, who was herself a fine singer as a chorister.

I was quite a good student, but I was certainly not an athlete. My father had been a keen football fan and my younger brother, George, was good at the game. But I remember my first game of football at school. I was in goal and George was Centre Forward for the opposing side. He scored six goals. I beat him up when we got home. My father beat me for beating my brother – and I gave up football. No, I am not a great games player.

Of course at that time only a small percentage of children had the chance of going to school. So when I say that I was poor, this is relative to the children who were actually in the school; I was much more fortunate than many. But in the mission schools I went to, the children of the teachers were allowed free schooling, so we were in a sense scholarship boys. We were the ones who had one shirt when the other people had three.

TASTE OF POLITICS

I did not become a priest. I became a teacher. Takoradi, along with Cape Coast, is one of the oldest educational centres of Ghana, with many schools and colleges, deriving from early mission activity. By now I was a young man with a wife and five children: Veronica, Irene, Carol, Peter and Iris, and I settled in Takoradi and became a teacher. English and History were my subjects, and during these years I taught in many of the leading schools of the area – Takoradi Secondary School, Sekondi College and, later, in the Ghana School of Journalism. But, whether I was a pupil or a teacher, I still seemed to find that life outside could be more instructive than the classroom, and more interesting. It was in fact the motto of my old school, The Washington Carver Institute, which seemed to me to tell the truth: 'We learn not for school but for life' – and so it was my activities outside the classroom that occupied most of my attention, and, I always say, really completed my education. Because of that first contact with the British Communist Party I began to receive information from a number of international political organizations and to be invited, regularly, to attend courses and seminars in all parts of the world. I was written to by the International Union of Students, by the World Federation of Democratic Youth, by the World Federation of Trades Unions, the World Peace Council and many others. And although the British Colonial Government did not approve, I went on many of these courses – I travelled widely in Eastern Europe, to Czechoslovakia, to Hungary, to East Germany – and even as far afield as Cuba.

It was not easy to make these trips, because the Colonial Government kept a close watch on people like myself who had declared Communist or Socialist sympathies, and frequently made it difficult for us to leave the country. Although we were usually invited as part of a team or delegation, belonging to, say, the student movement, or the youth movement, or the trades union movement, exit visas were only secured with great difficulty and usually with some delay. On one occasion at least, my passport was seized and I was forbidden to leave the country, but there were ways and means, and the overland routes through Togo and the Ivory Coast were used regularly. I made many good friends on these trips abroad, both among those I travelled with and among those we met at the conferences. On my first ever visit to Eastern Europe, for example, my companion was Anthony Kobina-Woode, who was as active in Trade Union organization as I was in the Student Movement. Tony, as we all called him, became, during the Nkrumah years, the General Secretary of the Trades Union Movement, and later on became a very successful businessman, the Managing Director of the First National Insurance Corporation of Ghana. He is a self-made, man a very fine and capable leader; of all the people I know, I consider his thinking about public life and politics to be closest to my own. It is also a great pleasure to have been able to persuade such a very strong friend to come and buy land in my own area of Manya Krobo, and to become a farmer there.

But the people I met on these travels and at these conferences and seminars, were also a source of friendship. They were all part of the international socialist movement; they were all, like myself at that time, young and beginning their active careers; and they were, many of them, to remain friends and colleagues in the years to come. There were so many of them I recall, Berlinguer, the former General Secretary of the Italian Communist Party, Augustino Neto, later the President of Angola, Ruth First, recently so tragically killed, Amilcar Cabral, who was assassinated in Conakry, Chedi Jagan and his wife Ruth – and, of course, Fidel Castro and Che Guevara, who I met on many occasions and who became I may say a great friend of mine.

The events in British Guiana during this period increased the obsession of the British, expressed both publicly in the press and privately in Government circles, with the threat of international communism.

And so some of us were the price that Nkrumah paid for his temporary respectability, and we were expelled from the Convention Peoples Party. We were regarded in an unspoken way, as political outlaws, and on several occasions, for example, I was brought back by French Police from Togo or from Abidjan and delivered to the hands of the Special Branch in Accra. Not that I was, or any of us were, imprisoned or in any formal sense political prisoners; we were just under observation and prevented from taking any active part in political life. As yet another gendarme handed me over at Accra Airport, I remember one of the white policemen saying 'Bloody Communist'. That was just about the level of understanding.

In this sort of political atmosphere, it was not only impossible to remain a member of the CPP, it was equally impossible to remain a teacher in Government service, and I was dismissed. And so, after nearly seven years in Takoradi as a teacher, I was without a job. I needed a job and was lucky enough to be appointed Manager of the Ringway Hotel in Accra, a new hotel, just opened, belonging to Mr Akufo Addo. Akufo Addo, who later became Chief Justice of Ghana was a man of great integrity and honesty, and he did not believe, he used to say, in rumours – only in evidence. He told me that he did not mind if people said I was a communist, or even if I actually was a communist; provided that none of these things affected the efficient running of the hotel or the success of the business. In fact, politics – if not myself personally – brought some good business to the Ringway Hotel during my time there. Diplomatic relations were established between Ghana and the Soviet Union, and before the USSR Embassy was built, the staff of the newly opening Embassy established themselves at the Ringway Hotel and provided both a good income and a great deal of political discussion as well!

I had been a teacher and I had been a journalist but this was the first time I had been involved in the world of business, and I still think that working as a manager at the Ringway was the most interesting job I have had in my life. It was a management job with a lot of complex and competing demands being made on me, and as the first African to be appointed as a manager at the Ringway, which was the first international hotel to be built in the country, it was a special challenge to me. I worked hard, both at the administration and at the task of making sure the customers were happy, at the same time I took correspondence courses for the examinations of the Institute of Hotel management, and I became qualified in the job. And I did well. I was paid £90 a month, more than a reasonably senior civil servant in those days. I lived in a flat in the hotel (where my family, who had remained in Takoradi, could visit me). I had free food and very cheap drink. It was, in fact, an enjoyable as well as a challenging life, and as the hotel trade is a gregarious business. I met many people and made many friends. Among those who used to come to the hotel at that time and with whom I became friendly, were Kwabena Tufouh, G.T. Oddoye, Senior Civil Servants Johnny Quashie-Idun, Justice Robert Hayfron-Benjamin, William Ofori Atta, Alhaji Kwaw Swanzy, and Justice Roger Korsah, all Accra lawyers – a few names among many.

ACTIVE IN POLITICS

Tawia Adamafio was an important political figure, and one whom I got to know very well at this time. He was then General Secretary of the CPP, and was Minister for Presidential Affairs, so he kept me in touch with the political thinking and with the affairs of the Government. He also arranged for me to give regular commentaries on political matters on Radio Ghana after the news broadcasts in the afternoon, and these talks of 5-7 minutes duration, I gave almost every other day for nearly two years. I was for the first time in my life a businessman, but I still felt the need to express my views on the world outside. And then one day Tawia Adamafio came in and asked me to become the Principal Research Officer at the Bureau of African Affairs – a title which included being the editor of the monthly magazine *Voice of Africa*. The Bureau of African Affairs had been started by George Padmore, but after his death Nkrumah had taken it under his own wing, and the Bureau of African Affairs now reported direct to the President. Clearly I could not refuse, and almost immediately I was plunged into the middle of the propaganda machine which was spreading Kwame Nkrumah's views to the whole of Africa.

Nkrumah's vision of the defeat of colonialism, of the achievement of true, economic, independence by the African, was not limited to Ghana. From the first, and quite openly and logically, he concerned himself with the affairs of other parts of Africa – countries where he considered Ghana could provide an example or give a lead, or give aid. Every month in *The Voice of Africa*, we discussed the problems of colonial Africa, of specific problems in specific countries, and copies were delivered (100,000 was the minimum print run) to all parts of the continent. We were banned in many countries still under colonial rule, but we managed to reach most countries by one means or another. The distribution system of *the Voice of Africa* was in fact one of the largest and most ingenious distribution systems that could be imagined, and no frontier was safe!

When I was in Accra, I was writing, but much of the job that I had to do involved travel. Nkrumah's all-Africa view involved practical help as well as verbal, and the guerilla camps which were established in certain parts of Ghana were the responsibility of our unit, and the people who were trained and the arms and materials that were sent had to be visited and checked up on. Certain aspects of this exercise was my job, there were other functions of the Bureau which were directly under A K Barden. As the struggle in Africa intensified my aspect of the exercise was granted full autonomy. I travelled officially as a journalist. I travelled continuously. I travelled throughout West Africa. I went to Kenya, Tanganyika, Zanzibar, to the Congo and Angola, to all those countries where there was a liberation movement slowly developing and where the prospects of Independence were on the horizon. I travelled to talk about the detailed political planning for the future of some of them. I remembered helping former President Ghoukouni Weddeye of Chad to form a political movement in Chad. Although I have not kept a detailed record, I know I made, for example, twenty-eight trips in 1960, the first year of this activity, alone. And this activity, like my earlier international travels, brought me into contact with a whole generation of political leaders who were just emerging. I met Obote, both in Uganda and at the Ugandan Constitutional Conference in London – and in particular his brilliant young supporter John Kakonge and Attorney General Binaisa. I met Kaunda, and Nyerere, Oscar Kambona, Dr Hastings Banda, Humphrey Mulemba, Munu Sipalo, Oginga Odinga, Oliver Tambo, Walter Sisulu, Nelson Mandela, Robert Mugabe, Eduardo Mondlane Jawara, Joshua Nkomo, Amilcar Cabral, Wallace Johnson, Siaka Stevens, Harry Nkubula, and Simon Kapwepwe. I worked closely with a whole generation of leaders, slipping across the border when I could not enter the country legally, and suffering the excitements and risks which went with this sort of activity. I was beaten up in Lagos and banned from entering Nigeria, thrown out of Senegal, and interned in Madrid. It was a demanding job!

This system of writing and publishing, combined with active

political support for Independence Movements, was continued when Nkrumah founded *The Spark* in 1962, which was intended to be, and became, a bigger and more forceful *Voice of Africa*.

The same pattern of work which had developed at the *Voice of Africa* continued with *The Spark*. I would travel, keeping only the writing of the editorial to myself, on my return. All the other work, the putting together of the rest of the paper, was in the hands of S G Ikoku, who was the co-editor. Known as 'S.G.' to everyone, he was the pillar of our organization, and would, at high speed, convert all the news I brought from my travels into the pages of *The Spark*.

We invited a few friends from Britain, Joan and Ron Bellamy and Denis Ogden, who became fully involved with the production of the paper. They contributed a lot in building *The Spark*, and contributing to Party education. I always treasure my relation with them. They are my very good friends.

The newly independent countries of Africa gradually sorted themselves out into two groups, the progessive and the conservative – called the Casablanca Group and the Monrovia Group, after the names of the locations of where the two conferences were held in 1961. The need to bring these two groups together was paramount, and fitted in with Kwame Nkrumah's vision of a United Africa. Our job on *The Spark* was to crystallize Nkrumah's thinking in terms of specific policies and to describe the issues of each week in ways which reflected his thinking; thus, in particular his general and often non-specific Pan Africanism was reflected in our leaders and our articles as moves to get the two separate groups of African nations to work together. Similarly, when we were sent on missions or to conferences throughout Africa, we not only travelled with a specific task in hand – to encourage a treaty, or to organize groups to fight against colonialism – but we worked at the same time, in every way we could and in every country, towards an organization that would reflect the possibility of a United Africa. And from this came the Organization of African Unity, formed at the great meeting in Addis Ababa in May 1963.

Throughout the years of change and debate, the 1950s and 1960s, some of us thought that Kwame Nkrumah made too many compromises and did not consistently appear as the leader of the radical wing in Pan-African affairs. That long period of transition from complete colonial government through internal self-government to independence that Ghana passed through – by far the longest period of peaceful transition in any African country – was bound to lead to criticism from the left and it did. Looking back, historians are now beginning to show how well Nkrumah played the political game; it is also possible to see how slow he was to come to terms with the extreme left – and how he was more completely of the left in his final exile than he had ever been when in Ghana and in power.

Dr Felix Moumie, a very good friend of mine, was a leader of the left in the Camerouns. He spent some time in Ghana when he was organizing the guerilla movement in the Camerouns after independence. As we were both on the left we got on very well, but it became apparent that he was well to the left of Nkrumah who, indeed, suspected some of his actions at certain stages. It was unfortunate that he was killed in Europe before his stand could crystallize.

In what might be called the Padmore period, Nkrumah was very close to Tom Mboya, who was then Chairman of the All African Peoples Conference, and known to be anti-communist (oddly, Nkrumah later became a great friend of Mboya's opponent, Oginga Odinga). But it was George Padmore who defined the anti-communist theme in Pan-Africanism. The ideas of Marxism were so useful and convenient to some of the proponents of Pan-Africanism that they had inevitably become associated with it. It helped the arguments; it greatly strengthened the anti-imperialist posture. Padmore showed that it was possible to be anti-imperialist without necessarily being communist, and he gathered distinguished disciples from all parts of the Pan-Africanist movement to this point of view – and indeed at that time Nkrumah himself expressed sympathy for this position – at least publicly. It is important to recognize the two strands in the independence movements in Africa; that of nationalist Pan-Africanism, and that of Marxist Pan-

Africanism. These two themes ran throughout the politics of the period and one would dominate in the affairs of one country at one time for a while and then be superseded by the other. In the South African Liberation Movement one was broadly represented by the Pan-African Congress and the other by the African National Congress. But in general the more moderate organization, the Pan-African Congress which had its office in Accra (as opposed to the African National Congress, operating out of Dar es Salaam and London) was the organization the Bureau of African Affairs associated itself with – indeed Peter Rabiroko, the publicity secretary of the PAC was one of the Associate Editors on the *Voice of Africa*, and Robert Sobukwe, of the PAC was more acceptable to Ghana in those years than the greatly distinguished Albert Luthuli. Nelson Mandela, for example, did not get as much support, as an ANC man, from the Bureau of African Affairs, as he would have had otherwise, and eventually he told me he was being messed around so much by these conflicts and by A K Barden (who took over the administration of the Bureau after the death of Padmore), that he was going back to South Africa to fight. I kept my close relation with him and Oliver Tambo. Throughout, a lot of new independence and revolutionary organizations were being formed in Southern Africa and they all took the pattern of the ANC or PAC.

At *The Spark*, we moved steadily throughout these years to the left and towards organizations like the ANC, with its stronger anti-imperialist stand. It became increasingly clear to us that the position defined by George Padmore provided nothing to contain the flood of Pan-Africanist springs that were bursting out all over Africa. That flood could only be contained and channelled, we decided, by radical ideas – and it became the policy of *The Spark* to develop and propagate these ideas.

Nkrumah knew, as we did, that it was no good just saying 'Africa must unite'. It was essential that proper reasons were found and demonstrated to the people, why Africa should unite; and this was why Nkrumah founded *The Spark*. He knew that the movement he was promoting must have a sound ideological basis and that it should be seen to have such a basis. He also knew that although more than most people active in politics, he was able to keep his eyes on a distant goal at the same time as dealing with the dramas and crises of every day. He needed a strategic cell, as it were, to draw out his ideas and make them specific in terms of the main aim of his politics. So he evolved the working relationship which bound Ikoku Habib Nyiang, Bello and myself and the staff of *The Spark* so closely to him. We called him the 'Editor-in-chief', and we were at all times very close to him; but he knew that without the discusions – and the arguments – that he had with us he would not be able to develop his ideas in the way that he wanted. He would call us, sometimes late at night, to come and talk with him; sometimes it was an early morning walk, before the work of the day began. But I think Ikoku and myself were able to put our point of view to him, throughout this period, and argue with him about some of his conclusions we were not happy with. Professor Kojo Abraham was a silent worker in the group. A distinguished academic and a sober minded man who sometimes argued with me if he thought we were going to the extremes, I respected his views on all issues in those days and always kept him before me as a future leader of Ghana.

So *The Spark* was the ideological organ of the CPP. I was also involved myself to some extent in the ordinary day-to-day politics of Ghana at this time. We would attack, in the Journal, a Minister who we felt was deviating from the right path; we would launch a discussion of a new direction which it was agreed the Government should take; we would, as an Editorial Team, attend the annual Party Conference and comment on decisions reached. But our discussions of local politics were always on the ideological level. Through all the weekly battles of the politicians; our eyes were on the horizon.

The purpose of *The Spark* was summarized by Kwame Nkrumah himself when he wrote a survey of its work in our 100th issue in November 1964:

In 1957 the Gold Coast attained political independence, and Ghana was born. This new nation was conceived as a prototype of the new Africa. I see the new Africa as one vast reconstructed society rising from the ruins of imperialism, colonialism and neo-colonialism and spreading over the mountains, valleys, cities and hamlets with its people firmly united by bonds of humanism and egalitarianism.

The first task of Ghana was to help the anti-colonial struggle everywhere in Africa. At midnight on March 6th, 1957, as the Union

Jack was lowered for the last time in these parts and the new flag of Ghana with the lodestar of Africa fluttered in the evening breeze, I declared that 'the independence of Ghana is meaningless unless it is linked with the total liberation of Africa!

Ever since, Ghana has worked assiduously to achieve this objective. In pursuit of this goal, we immediately arranged for two Conferences – the Conference of Independent African States and the All African Peoples' Conference which were successfully held in Accra in 1958.

At that time, there were only eight independent states in Africa. By 1963 the number had risen to thirty-two. The drive to free the African Continent from colonialism had yielded rich dividends.

I must, however, point out that the de-colonization of Africa has been helped on by two trends. These trends, though agreed on the need to liquidate colonialism, are nonetheless antithetical in their aims. The first trend – the national liberation movement – derives its motive force from the African masses and sees the termination of colonisalism as the first step, the political condition, to the complete elimination of imperialism from the African continent. The second trend was set in motion by the imperialist powers. The aim has been to accommodate the demands of the African peoples for independence without relaxing the grip of imperialism over the wealth of Africa. The result has been the setting up of states which are politically independent but which remain economically and militarily dependent on the former colonial powers. This is what I have described as neo-colonialism.

It has therefore become imperative to open a new phase of the African Revolution. Neo-colonialism now has to be unmasked and defeated. And neo-colonialism is a much more dangerous enemy than colonialism. For under a neo-colonialist regime, imperialism sheds the odium of direct alien rule but retains all the advantages of economic and military control.

The struggle against neo-colonialism is an integral part of our peoples efforts directed at national reconstruction. Indeed, the two processes are but the two sides of the same coin. There is a direct correlation between national reconstruction and the struggle against neo-colonialism. For fundamental economic changes can proceed only where the old economic relations of imperialism are destroyed. And what is true of the economic sector is also true of all fields of national life.

The destruction of neo-colonialism and the building of a new social order in its place cannot be achieved by merely wishing it. This requires certain conditions for its full and rapid realization. And the two key conditions for its realization are African unity and socialism.

African unity – by which we mean the political unification of the African continent made manifest in a Union Government for all Africa – is the political framework within which the process of liquidating neo-colonialism can proceed apace. It is the political condition for decolonization of the rest of colonialism in its place. It is the political condition for the early and complete break-up of the bastion of international finance capital in the southern portion of the African continent.

The other condition – socialism – defines the new social order that must replace the imperialist system of colonialism, neo-colonialism, racism and apartheid. Any attempt to destroy colonialism or neo-colonialism without putting something new and better in its place will only lead to a recrudescence of imperialism in one form or another.

The two conditions outlined above coalesce into one condition precedent for building the new Africa – a new ideology. The new ideology must be scientifically formulated. It must be vigorously propagated. For a united people armed with an ideology which explains the status quo and illumines out path of development is the greatest asset we possess for the total liberation and complete emancipation of Africa. And the emancipation of Africa completes the process of the emancipation of man.

These are the considerations that lie behind my decision to found *The Spark*. The new Africa needs a new ideology socialist in content and continental in outlook. The propagation of such an ideology demands an ideological journal or journals serving all Africa. Hence *The Spark*.

A movement without an ideology is lost from its inception. If it flounders from situation to situation without a clear guide, without an understanding of the laws of social development it cannot give that clear uncompromising lead which the complexities of modern politics demand. Similarly a movement without a paper, fights with one hand tied behind its back, and we see our function as expressing the practical and ideological aims and tasks of the movement for the complete liberation of Africa, for continental union government and for socialism in this great continent.

In the words of our very first issue, 'We are committed to the struggle for the total liberation and unity of Africa. We hope to discuss through our columns the problems of the socialist revolution in Africa'. We humbly submit that we are bent on fulfilling this commitment. To our friends all over Africa and in the rest of the world we send our warmest greetings. *The Spark* has kindled a flame: the flame which will guide us to total liberation, unity and socialism.'

I published some of the main themes we discussed in *The Spark* some time later in a book called *Some Essential Features of Nkrumahism*. But perhaps my contacts with the Russians during the 1960s might give an example of the sort of ideological work we were involved in. I made several trips to the Soviet Union in the 1960s to visit my opposite numbers on *Pravda*, the first visit being in 1962 and the last in 1965. I became a close friend during these visits with Pavel Satyukov, the Editor-in-Chief of *Pravda*, and the 1965 visit was to launch a formal discussion with Rumyantsev, who took over from Satyukov in 1964, to attempt to answer a question that was concerning Nkrumah and ourselves: 'How do you transform a mass party into an ideological party?'

In the struggle for Independence, in Ghana and in other African countries as well, everyone is united against the colonial power. People of all opinions, of all backgrounds, join together in the struggle to get rid of the enemy. In this unity is forged a single party state, but after independence when the unifying enemy has gone, it is revealed slowly but steadily, that the different elements of the party that has achieved independence, have no common ideological objectives. The problem is easy to solve, said the Russians. Just as in Eastern Europe you could take the Anti-Fascist fronts and turn them into positive, ideologically oriented, communist parties. We did this after the Second World War, said the Russians, you can do this in Africa. I had to point out to Satyukov and his companions, however, that the major difference between Eastern Europe in the 1940s and Africa, lay in the armies. The presence of Soviet troops encouraged the developments they spoke of in Eastern Europe. In Africa – and certainly in Ghana — the army in newly independent countries was a section of society not sympathetic to the new system of government, in training, in sympathy, and in self-interest the men who controlled the armed forces were certainly not going to be in favour of the development of socialist parties. So our positions were stated, and were quite different – we had good evidence that following the Russian line was not the right thing to do, and it was, as a matter of interest agreed that representatives from *The Spark*, from *Pravda*, and from the Cairo paper *Al Ahram* would meet in February of the next year, 1966, to try to reach agreement on the correct course of action for Africa. We never met: the military coup of January in Ghana unfortunately proved that my analysis of the situation was correct.

I must mention that in January 1965 when Ernesto Che Guevara visited Ghana, I had the opportunity of discussing the same subject with him in my home. He said, and I quote him verbatim from a tape recorded statement we later published:

To turn a mass party into a party of cadres is a relatively simple affair as far as its formal aspects are concerned, but the execution of such a change inevitably carries with it the need for changes in the mentality of the leadership of the party as a whole, and in many cases, also a physical change of previous personalities of the mass party. It also requires a general drive in the education, selection and development of new cadres. This task may be obstructed by various kinds of mistakes. Among these I shall mention particularly the mistake which existed in the Cuban situation until the beginning of 1962, which we have called 'sectarism'. This situation was brought about, more than anything else, by the lack of definitions in the real tasks of the party within the state. The fundamental aspects in the change towards a party of cadres are the characteristics of the militant. In a mass party, a militant only has to accept a broad general line of action and be subject to a very general sort of discipline. In a party of cadres, every one of its members should accept being subject to an effective control of his ideological activity, and even of his private life. This is a very important difference and for this reason a very careful selection of cadres should be made before proceeding to a re-organization of the party structure.'

So the problem of creating an ideological party in a new state was not solved, and in the sense that it is also the problem of the one party state, Africa has still not solved it today. Country after country has adopted the one-party system, with full approval of the Russian ideologues, and they have failed to make it work. The same thing happened in Ghana when Nkrumah adopted the one-party system in 1964; there was no general agreement among the leaders of the party, never mind in the country at large, about the direction the nation was taking. So how, in this situation, is it possible to say that everyone is a member of one party, and that only one party exists? Those who had been working for the party since it came into being were not agreed amongst themselves; those who were forcibly coralled into the same organization by this piece of legislation were only slightly more amazed to discover that all Ghanaians were one. The legislation establishing a one party state, and the elections of 1965 which followed, were a good example of political action preceding instead of following, the establishment of an ideological framework. I was very unhappy about it. I think I had then the distinctive feeling that I have now that (they are the words of Winston Churchill): 'Many forms of government have been tried in this world of sin and woe. No one pretends that democracy is perfect or all-wise. Indeed, it has been said that democracy is the worst form of government, except for all those other forms that have been tried from time to time.'

The result of the elections under the one party system in Ghana in 1965 was that I became an MP: a single candidate from the CPP was nominated for each constituency and I was nominated – and elected, of course – for my home area of Asesewa. However uneasy I felt about the course we were taking, the one thing I did do in the remaining year of the Nkrumah and CPP rule was to turn myself into what might be called 'a constituency MP'. I may have been nominated and I may have been the only candidate, but I was determined to let the people of my constituency know that I was their Member of Parliament, and I worked hard at getting to know the people in my constituency and I worked, I think I can say, as hard as anyone could at the problems of the area. I was not an MP for very long – the military coup came in February 1966 – but I must have had some effect on the region; years later, when military rule was withdrawn in 1981, all the candidates in my region to whom I gave my support publicly, were elected.

Without either democracy or an ideology, the country had no chance, and in a sense the people knew it. Publicly, people were afraid to criticize the party – at least at first – privately the jokes, the irony – and the criticism that these implied – were always there, and it was these characteristics in the population at large that in turn gave rise to the feeling of unease that took over the country. Very soon after my own election as an MP, I met an old friend, Mallace-Addow in my home town who said laughingly 'Have you collected your first month's salary yet? I hope you are going to give it to me – after all, you had no campaign expenses to bear'. The lightheartedness did not conceal the criticism; and the criticisms grew.

All through these years we were working with the complex nature of Kwame Nkrumah. An example of this nature of his personality occurred in late 1965. A senior officer at the Bureau of African Affairs went to Nkrumah and reported that K A Gbedemah had been killed in Lomé. Remember that from being one of Nkrumah's closest friends and associates, Gbedemah had become one of his fiercest critics: and just as no critic is so fierce as one who has changed sides, so no enemy was in public more strongly attacked than was Gbedemah by the Ghanaian papers. When the report of the death came in, Nkrumah called some of the editors of the press to his office and told us what had been said. I saw that he was obviously and clearly upset. There were tears on his face, and as he stood at the window he used his handkerchief; his words were: 'He shouldn't have died, he had contributed a lot'. As he was at the same time a man of action, Nkrumah asked us to check whether the report was true, and eventually it turned out that it was not. Gbedemah was alive and well and in Europe, and the report from Lomé was mysteriously inaccurate. The man who had reported with such anticipated pleasure the false news was relieved of his post, and Gbedemah remained a political enemy. But what I remember now is the instinctive humanity of Kwame Nkrumah's reaction – it was that of a man who, when his opponent Dr R E G Armattoe died, called the press and asked for moderation. Kwame Nkrumah never signed a death warrant; I know that well, as I shared a prison block later on with many who owed their lives to this unwillingness to condemn. When Sylvanus Olympio was killed in Togo, an old opponent of Nkrumah's died, I was out of Accra at the time and *The Spark* appeared with the headline 'An Imperialist Tool is Killed' and with a crude and vicious cartoon. Nkrumah saw an early copy from the run, ordered printing to be stopped and the 40,000 copies that had already been run off were destroyed. '*The Spark* is not a local unimportant paper,' he said. 'When someone dies in Africa it is to be deplored.' And the copies of *The Spark* that were finally issued recorded Olympio's death in a proper manner. Nkrumah retained a firm grip on affairs, remained very close to *The Spark*, the paper he had founded, and certainly bore no permanent malice to his political opponents.

THE AFRICAN STRUGGLE

I undertook several missions for Kwame Nkrumah. Uganda, for example, was a country I visited quite a number of times, and I was particularly involved in the period just before Uganda's Independence in 1961. Kwame Nkrumah had sent me to Obote to discuss the future constitution of Uganda and the structure of its independence, on a number of occasions. The greatest problem for Obote, and for Uganda, was to find a way of integrating the regions of Uganda into a united and independent Uganda. Obote's new and modern mass party was the dominant political force in the country but it was clear to most outsiders that any constitutional arrangements which ignored the powerful influence of the Kabaka of Buganda would not be a satisfactory solution. So Nkrumah sent me to discover the feeling of the people of Uganda, informally, and to provide another point of view from that of Obote himself. I entered Uganda as a journalist, and although closely questioned by the immigration officials, I was admitted. I went straight to the house of a good friend, John Kakonge, a brilliant and intelligent man who was later Minister of Economic Development – and later still one of Amin's victims. I discussed the Uganda problem, the question of their loyalty to Obote, with Kakonge and with his friends. We met Binaisa who became a very good friend of mine over the years, and who became Attorney General under Obote and himself became President briefly after the fall of Dr. Lule. Kakonge and Binaisa convinced me that there must be a formula of compromise between the forces of Obote and those of the Kabaka – and that the satisfactory solution might be for the Kabaka to be made Governor-General and Obote to be Prime Minister. So I left Kampala, without having seen Obote, or without Obote knowing I was in the country, and returned to Accra with a clear idea of the complexities of the country's political situation – and of the opportunities. As chance would have it, when I arrived at my home in Accra, two good friends of the same political persuasion arrived the same day: Dr Kwamena Ocran, later Minister of Health under Dr Limann arrived from Prague and Alao Aka Bashurun, President of WASU arrived from Lagos. We talked, the three of us, all night, and devised a formula which we could put to Nkrumah and which as it turned out we found a way of putting in an acceptable form, to Obote. As a result of this, I was asked to be in close touch with Obote's delegation to the Ugandan Constitutional Conference in London and was able to play an active part in securing the constitutional settlement which was reached. The Ghanaian influence on the solution was a strong one, with Kwesi Armah, then High Commissioner in London, being consulted at all stages and Dr Ekow Daniels, later Kwame Nkrumah's Deputy Attorney-General, and Minister of the Interior under President Limann, acting as the legal and academic adviser from his position at Professor Allot's department at the School of Oriental and African Studies, in London. And our formula for Uganda worked for a while. We managed to put together a package bringing the different forces in Uganda into a harmonious relationship – and this brief taste of success made the failure of the system a few years later seem all the more tragic. We had helped to establish a peaceful independent country in Africa, we had helped to install a progressively inclined Government in power, and we had arranged and grouped the progressive forces of Uganda. It seemed to be Pan-Africanism at work in the most practical way. But Kwame Nkrumah never stopped warning us of the dangers that Pan-Africanism was facing, and he was right. No one could have been sorrier than I at the tragic way in which Uganda seems to have lost its path.

There were certain aspects of the Zimbabwe struggle I should mention. I happened to be in Central and Southern Africa in December 1961, when Sir Edgar Whitehead banned the NDP which was being led by Joshua Nkomo, Robert Mugabe, Leopold Takawira and others. Two hundred and fifty three leaders and officials of the NDP were served with orders under the Native Affairs Act 'prohibiting them from entering any tribal area other than those in which they have land rights!' Fifty-one others received orders under the Law and Order (maintainance) Act. It prohibited them from attending political party rallies for three months.

I remember Takawira and Robert Mugabe saying that though they were served with the restrictions they were free to operate in other political groupings because they enjoyed no land rights.

Joshua Nkomo's view was that they must form another organisation immediately. On the 17 of December 1961, the Zimbabwe African Peoples Union – ZAPU was formed. The ZAPU executive announced on that day comprised Joshua Nkomo, National President Dr Tichafa Parirenyatwa, the physician, his deputy, Rev. Ndabaningi Sithole, chairman, Booker T.W. Malianga, National Secretary, he was assisted by Aggripa Mkahlera, Clement Muchachi was the organiser, Robert Gabriel Mugabe, Publicity Director, the secretary for Pan African International Affairs was Leopold Takawira. Jane Mgwenya was given the position as Secretary for women and Joseph Msika was Secretary for youth.

I was sorry two friends of mine in the NDP – George Silundika and Moton Malianga were dropped from the leadership of ZAPU. The view was held that George was unpopular with the rank and file of the movement. Robert Mugabe was of the opinion that Moton could not fit into the change of things because he appeared lazy. I knew Moton was almost always late for meetings. I grew to like Moton in 1960 when he and Mawema were put before the court. He was very courageous. I always thought he was very sincere. I saw the same trait in Enos Nkala who held the reputation as the longest serving detainee at Sikonbela prison. It was quite clear in those days that Robert Mugabe would take over the leadership of the liberation movement. He saw very early and kept on saying that Joshua Nkomo's flair for constitutional conferences was wasting time. He opted for armed struggle.

The period showed the rise of nationalist movements in Central and Southern Africa. the Congo crisis was at its apogee and the Cha-Cha-Cha campaign of violence launched by the United National Independence Party led by Kenneth Kaunda in Northern Rhodesia was a great threat to the white settlers. The period coincided with the Sharpeville massacre in South Africa. The one-man-one-vote slogan had gained grounds and the strikes in Salisbury, Bulawayo, Gatooma, Gwelo and Que Que were significant signs of the struggle ahead.

It was clear that the ZAPU itself was going to split. Before I left Southern and Central Africa it was quite clear to me that Joshua Nkomo's view that ZAPU was to operate as a movement which was going to effect change by constitutional means was not going to hold the liberation movement together for a long time. The idea that all peaceful means had to be exhausted before one could contemplate bloodshed was not popular with the youth. One could feel the impatience for guerilla warfare in the air. Robert Mugabe, Leopold Takawira, Dr. Parirenyatwa, Moton Malianga and Reuben Mya Mureba from the Highfield were being vocal in the assertion that majority rule could be achieved through sabotage and violence being carried out against the white settlers. I was surprised when I realized that Rev. Sithole and Jason Moyo too held the same view.

A 'General Chedu' in Highfield was already operating with petrol bombs, light arms from Cairo were already getting in through Shabani to Salisbury and it was not surprising that Robert Mugabe was always addressing rallies in Highfield.

I remember in those days, Ian Smith who later became kingpin of the white settlers struggle in Southern Africa was the most hated whiteman in Rhodesia. He was noted for singing an Afrikaans song "Bobojaan Klam de berg" – The Baboon climbs the mountain – at public rallies. He was hated by the Africans for that.

I reported all these incidents and gave the true colour of the changes taking place to Kwame Nkrumah.

I visited Zanzibar, which had just beome independent, because we were supporters of Abeid Karume, the leader of the Black African Party there – and I arrived on the day of the violent coup, led by John Okelo which overthrew the Arab rulers – 12 January 1964. Our Bureau of African Affairs had not been directly involved in the coup and it was a surprise to us, although a number of Karume's activists has been trained in Ghana. It was startling to arrive in the midst of such an event, and the amount of bloodshed was not to my taste. I did in fact attempt to say to Karume that I thought enough killing had taken place but his reply was 'My people have died, many of them, over the years – we must bring this to an end, now.' So the revolt against the Arabs, and the takeover was complete. The excitement as well as the bloodshed was remarkable – and I joined in the crowd who assembled at the Radio Station, which had been thrown open to celebrate the revolution. Anyone and everyone was invited to step forward to speak into the microphone and say what they thought about the events of the

day. It was an invitation I thought it better to refuse myself –
my role was to be a little more discreet!

But this event and the Zanzibar connection in general
showed one other strand in our involvement in international
affairs – that of Nkrumah and the Bureau of African Affairs. We
were concerned to help countries secure their independence, it
is true; but we were also concerned about countries where a
minority controlled the government or wielded excessive
power. The Arab minority in Zanzibar had had an unhealthy
stranglehold on the the life of the island – and the Sudan, and
Mozambique were both in their different ways, other examples
of parts of Africa where the overbearing power of a minority
had aroused the interest and concern of the Pan-Africanists.
The fiercest campaign that Nkrumah waged against a minority
regime was the fight against the Central African Federation. In
the context of his Pan-African ideals, Kwame Nkrumah saw
the Central African Federation of the two Rhodesias and
Nyasaland as a new South Africa in the making, and every
weapon should be used, he contended, to prevent an unnatural
minority rule from being entrenched in such a large area of the
Continent. Political pressure was what was used, and force and
arms were not ruled out.

Dr Hastings Banda, for example, was practising medicine as
a G.P. in Kumasi in Ghana, when Nkrumah himself called for
him and persuaded him to return to Nyasaland, to his country,
to take part in the independence process. Banda's return to
Nyasaland in 1958, his sweeping election victory in 1961, and
the independence of the new state of Malawi in 1964 were steps
all encouraged and aided by Ghana and by the Bureau of African Affairs, and were considered by us all as necessary steps in
the liberation of Africa, in the protection of Africa against
minority domination, and, in the longer term, in the freeing of
Africa from economic domination. But at the same time Hastings Banda himself showed up the difficulties of our programme. He was Nkrumah's friend and he owed a great deal to
Ghana's support and encouragement. When the OAU assembled in Accra in October 1965, and many countries did not
want to attend, black-balling Ghana, Banda came. But he was
straightforward and he was honest in his reaction to the
demands which we Pan-Africanists were making on him. 'You

are too soon' he said, 'for continental government'. He admitted openly that Malawi was more pleased with its independence than it could be concerned with continental unity. His attitude was, yes, we'll meet in Addis Ababa, or, yes, we'll listen to you talk – but, no, this is not practical politics at the present time. Banda spoke out, straightforwardly and indeed President Tsiranana of the Malagasy Republic cried 'It's all demagogy' at the Addis Ababa Conference of the OAU; but most sat and listened and did not dare react. I sat behind Nkrumah when he spoke to the OAU Conference in Addis Ababa in 1963 and I watched the faces of the leaders as he left his prepared script and pointing at each in turn, at Haile Sellassie, at Tafawa Balewa, at Modibo Kaita, at Maga; he said: 'If we do not come together, if we do not unite, we shall all be thrown out, all of us one by one – and I also will go'. He said 'The OAU must face a choice now – we can either move forward to progress through our effective African Union or step backward into stagnation, instability and confusion – an easy prey for foreign intervention, interference and subversion.' He got a standing ovation for that speech and although we felt he should have been calmer and that perhaps he had gone too far, his reaction was, 'Let me tell them, let me tell them'.

Nkrumah's words in Addis Ababa reflected the conflicting aims of his policy and of the Bureau of African Affairs. Our problem was: how could we bring together the aims of national Independence and of African unity? Kwame Nkrumah's concept of African unity emphasized the need for organizing African efforts on a continental scale. In the concept he terms the 'optimum zone of self-induced development' he postulated that as soon as an African state was born, there arose the need to protect the new political unit against internal and external enemies. In addition the new state must set out boldly to provide the basis for the fullest satisfaction of the material and cultural needs of the people. In short, the new state must expand its productive capacity many times over.

This need for an expansion of production, on which the fullest development of all hinged, demanded two conditions:

(a) the use of the most up-to-date technology; and

(b) an optimum area of development.

The optimum area of development is consequent on the use

of the most up-to-date technology for the fullest development of modern industrial technology – that is to say, the use of the largest and latest machines without carrying excess capacity – cannot be achieved until an optimum area within which development can be self-induced is secured.

Nkrumah therefore emphasized that the only other solution to this problem is the former colonial masters' forceful annexation of foreign markets. And how ludicrous, he said, to think that an African state can follow the path of development that postulates colonialism on condition of success.

In explaining the concept he said the optimium area of self-induced development must necessarily be a vast land mass with a big population. The vast land mass is required because a wide variety of geographical regions and geological formations is needed to yield all the agricultural and mineral products on which modern industrialization depends. A big population is needed in order to provide the various types of labour skills, and, even more important, the vast and expanding markets for the products for a highly technical industrial system.

Accordingly, the fullest development of our people in Africa demands the application of up-to-date technology which in turn implies an optimum area of development, if such development is to be self-induced.

The search for an optimum area of self-induced development leads inescapably to the African continent being considered as a single unit of development.

Nkrumah had looked at the United States, where he had been a student, and he had seen how a certain land mass contained within itself all the necessary economic conditions of labour, of skills, of capital, of minerals, of energy reserves – to provide a self-contained and self-development economy. He saw that Russia, the Eastern Bloc, provided a similar economic unity. He wanted Africa to provide another, for he saw that within Africa there were enormous skills, enormous assets and great potential. What was needed for true independence, Nkrumah argued, was that there should be a clear, recognized and agreed geographical expression of the area which desired its independence, and that this area should have the balanced resources necessary for self-sufficiency. The achievement of this self-conscious self-sufficiency 'became an area of resistance' to outside powers – in other words by the force of its own powers of development it becomes a great power. This, Nkrumah said, was what had happened to the USA and to the Soviet Union. This is what Great Britain had been, in association with its colonies; it had constructed its Empire to make an 'optimum zone of self-induced development', and when it had lost its Empire it was no longer a great power. It was this interpretation of course, which led us to attack the creation of the European Economic Community. Not that the underlying unconscious aims of the community were wrong, because in a sense the Europeans were seeking for that optimum zone for themselves in their own grouping, but that in creating associate status for some countries in Africa, as in the agreements for Associate membership as shown in Lomé 1 and Lomé 2, they were admitting that the area of Europe itself was not an optimum zone as defined, they were infiltrating the emerging optimum zone of Africa with their own externalized capitalist demands. The two failures of Europe, to us, were that it had not a balanced grouping of resources, and that it had no political will and destination – only an inconsequential Parliament. If Africa was to come together in the way that would make it a great power and keep its true independence from outside forces it must come together with a Continental Union Government which would provide economic policies and defence policies – all the attributes of a great power.

We therefore worked hard to emphasize that African Unity must be looked at as the strategy of total liberation and complete independence of Africa. We believed that on the ruins of colonial relations had to be built a new economic and social order which would at one and the same time sustain Africa's independence and bring a fuller life within reach of all Africans. Flowing logically from this, independent African states must come together in order further to attain complete independence by breaking down the control of colonialism in the spheres of national economy, national defence and culture.

Our view was that African Unity could not mean the usual intercourse between sovereign states. Such intercourse is a normal feature of civilized life and exists even between hostile states.

Some slight degree of trade, telecommunications contacts

etc, do not mean, and could not constitute African Unity. African Unity should mean something more. It should involve the co-ordination of vital spheres of national life. The struggle for African Unity should be built on the principle that in addition to respect for each other's independence, sovereignty and territorial integrity, vital aspects of national life must be co-ordinated.

We took time to explain that political union would not be forced at the expense of some nations and to the glorification of others. It is a union in the creation of which every participating state surrenders a bit of its sovereignty. No one state gains at the expense of the other. Rather, every state surrenders something to a bigger unit in which everyone is again represented. We said this has been the way in which human society itself has evolved. The family lost some rights to the patriarchy to the benefit of the family; the patriarchy lost to the tribe; the tribe to the nation; the nation to the state.

Ghana was attacked in certain quarters in Africa that if we really stood for African Unity why did we support the dismantlement of the inter-territorial organizations like the West African Currency Board, the West African Frontier Force, and the West African Cocoa Research Institute. We explained that those agencies served the colonial administration. They were not 'institutions of African Unity', as they were described. On the contrary, they were agencies meant to reduce the overhead costs of colonial administration, agencies created primarily to make colonialism function more efficiently. They could not therefore be used to serve independent African states.

One of the most difficult assignments we undertook at the Bureau of African Affairs was how to make the October 1965 OAU conference in Accra succeed. There was a move by a section of the Western world to get the OAU buried in Accra. Kwame Nkrumah was the target; the OAU must be made to collapse on his lap.

On 13 February 1965, thirteen French-speaking African States concluded a conference at Head of State and Government levels at Nouakchott, capital of the Republic of Mauritania. The countries were – Cameroun, the Central African Republic, Chad, Congo (Brazzaville), Dahomey, Gabon, Ivory Coast, Malagasy, Mauritania, Niger, Senegal, Togo and

Upper Volta. They rounded off their week long conference with a communique that announced the formation of the Organisation Commune Africaine et Malgache (OCAM), the aim of which was to strengthen 'the solidarity and co-operation between states of Africa and Malagasy within the framework of the OAU'. President Ould Daddah of Mauritania was elected head of the organization and it was decided the headquarters should be Yaounde (Cameroun). Another meeting was fixed for January 1966 in Antenanarivo (Malagasy).

The analysis of the Bureau of African Affairs was that the entente ran counter to the progressive trend toward continental unity in Africa, and it was therefore aimed at disrupting the OAU. Its ultimate objective must be to bring all Africa under the hegemony of US imperialism.

In a memorandum to President Nkrumah we stated that the calculation of the architects of the move was that the planting of the *Presence Française* in many African states would permit a diplomatic rapprochement between these states and the existing spheres of Anglo-US influence in Africa, and thus open the door to the crack-up of the OAU. And the downfall of the OAU would in turn open the road for the ascendency of US influence throughout Africa.

The plan must have looked neat and tidy. But to us the architects had lost sight of one cardinal factor. They had reckoned without the peoples of Africa. To them the role and will of the African peoples counted for little or nought. Our thesis was that the Nouakchott conference was part of the grand design of the US to convert all Africa into a vast neo-colonialist empire, another Latin America. We connected the Nouakchott meeting with what was happening in the CongoZaire at about the same time.

The OAU took the line of reconciliation of the warring factions in the Congo, and sought the political settlement of the Congo crises within an African context. This clearly did not square with US arrangements for the Congo. And pressure was quickly brought to bear on some African States to change their stand.

Nigeria flouted the OAU Line, and declared support for Tshombe's government. And in their communiqué after the conference the Nouakchott group called for 'Peace in the Congo

and aid for the legal government of President Kasavubu and
Moise Tshombe'. In the process they had let it be known that
they intended to challenge the OAU stand on the Congo.
President Senghor of Senegal, speaking of the Conference of
Thirteen, asserted that 'we insist on respect being shown to the
principles defined in its (OAU) charter'. But all indications
showed something else.

The point we emphasized at that stage was that the thirteen
French-speaking African States had come out in open defiance
of the OAU. They had formed a new grouping contrary to the
Addis Ababa recommendation that all blocks of African States
be dissolved. They had constituted themselves into a group to
deal with the Congo problem in open disregard of the fact that
the OAU had set up an ad hoc committee on the Congo. And as
if to underline what their intention was, some member states of
the grouping had let it be known that they intended to boycott
the September 1965 Accra summit of the OAU. Their pretext
was that African freedom fighters were resident in Ghana.
They forgot that when at Cairo, in July 1964, they unanimously
agreed to hold the third OAU summit in Accra in 1965, these
African freedom fighters had already been living in Ghana for
several years.

Our problem was how we could evolve a plan to make the
OAU conference succeed, and at the same time keep the
momentum of the liberation struggle on the continent of Africa.

The Spark was to come out to fight the new move on the continent. In our first comment on the Nouakchott Entente we made
a move to split the policy of the US and France. We established
the link between the OCAM group and US diplomacy. At the
Nouakchott conference many of the French-speaking African
leaders had shown an inclination towards Washington and a
weakening of their ties with Paris. They were so happy with the
change of alliance that President Tsiranana of Malagasy
claimed 'we are big enough now to look after ourselves and
stand up to anybody'.

But the question then arose, why had this switch away from
Paris to Washington taken place. *The Spark* analysed that in the
face of the challenge of the African revolution, France, under
President de Gaulle, had sought to develop a liberal policy
towards Africa. She called for an end to foreign intervention in

the Congo. She had decided to withdraw her garrisons and military bases from Africa. She had wound up the Union of Africa and Malagasy (UAM).

The consequence of de Gaulle's policy of 'a new formula' had been the political exposure of the reactionary régimes France had propped up in Africa. These leaders were frightened. And to defend themselves against the rising tide of popular demand they sought the support of the United States.

The Spark and the Bureau of African Affairs took the line of 'speaking to the people of Africa', and left the diplomatic work to the African Affairs secretariat which was part of the Ministry of Foreign Affairs and the President's Office.

I visited Nouakchott and managed to get to the heart of some of the decisions arrived at in the conference. I discovered that M Rothschild, Financial Adviser to the Belgian Foreign Ministry had been in Mauritania throughout the conference. With such a midwife the offspring could almost certainly turn out to be a monster. After M Rothschild had officiated over the labour of bringing forth the OCAM, Mr 'Soapy' Mennen Williams, the USA Assistant Secretary of State for Africa was present at the delivery.

I reported to Kwame Nkrumah that the situation was quite serious. A senior Mauritanian Minister who held our view confided to me that the strategy was to smash the OAU; the tactic was to achieve it by trying to isolate one of its most loyal and vigorous supporters, Ghana. Through attacks and counter-attacks they hoped to split the OAU and render it ineffective and rent apart by internal strife.

I discovered that the charge made in February 1965 that Ghana was harbouring subversives and encouraging subversion was followed up with allegations of our complicity in the attempt on the life of President Diori of Niger. On the well-known principle that if enough mud was flung some might stick, they screamed the accusations from Nouakchott.

Before it was officially announced I reported that to consolidate the propaganda campaign the OCAM was to send a roving Presidential group composed of Presidents Yameogo of Upper Volta, Houphouet-Boigny of Ivory Coast, and Diori of Niger to visit other African states. As a first move President Yameogo visited the United States and launched an attack on some African countries, including Ghana. He announced that OCAM members would not be attending the summit in Accra.

Ghana had to launch a diplomatic offensive. We succeeded in getting President Maga of Dahomey to play a useful part in the exercise. I visited Dahomey with Dr Alex Quaison Sackey, then Ghana's Ambassador at the UN, and Nana Kobina Nketsia, to discuss aspects of our strategy with him. He was very frank with us.

We were forced to remove some of the freedom fighters from Accra, and temporarily accommodated the view of some of the states of 'moderate nationalism'. We narrowed our fight for unity to:

(1)   the immediate termination of colonial rule in Africa, and

(2)   the building up of a new economic and social order serving the interests of the broad masses.

We added our struggle against neo-colonialism after the conference started its work. In fact, Kwame Nkrumah was able to talk to the leaders of OCAM when he said: 'When I cast my eyes across the corridors of time and see the greatness of the coming events in Africa, I heave a deep sigh of relief, for I see clearly the irresistible forces of African nationalism rolling before them the remnants of colonialism rolling and crushing definitely the forces of reaction.

'Sometimes I am amazed at the lack of understanding on the part of some African leaders who think in terms of a sectionalized Africa, permanently balkanized and exploited by those who want to keep Africa divided.

'In this mid-twentieth century Africa can no longer remain the footstool of any foreign power. When I am accused by stooges of interfering in the internal affairs of other African countries, my answer is that every true African nationalist has a duty to concern himself with the present-day problems facing Africa.'

The OAU summit took place in Accra, and it was a great success.

In the Bureau of African Affairs we regarded ourselves as being the factory of the ideas of Kwame Nkrumah. It was our job to take his ideas, turn them into actuality – and to create the

Africa he imagined before it was too late. It is sad that most of the African leaders fell and the African states lost their immediate hope of true independence in the way that Nkrumah had forecast at Addis Ababa in 1964. Even Nkrumah's Ghana lost the momentum.

Thus, from one aspect of our enthusiasm there came the source of one of the major criticisms of the Bureau of African Affairs. Our first objective was to secure the independence of individual African countries, on the path to independence of Africa as a whole. But we were also struggling to effect changes in Government of those independent countries in Africa of whom we disapproved, whose attitudes were not progressive or whose actions were contrary to our view of the right course for Africa. These activities and this policy were, of course, used by those who overthrew Nkrumah to justify their coup. What few realized, and still fewer remembered, was that in the preamble to the Charter of the Organization of African Unity, the objectives were stated as being to fight not only colonialism, but neo-colonialism and apartheid – and we quoted this often in *The Spark* in our editorials to justify action against those regimes which, quite evidently, were the agents of neo-colonialism, and therefore barriers to the movement for African unity. Few of the leaders who subscribed to the Charter realized the full implication of its words. We stated that we were not interfering in other states' affairs. We were fighting neo-colonialism which could only be found in African states which had achieved formal independence.

These activities of the Bureau of African Affairs contributed to our becoming, in our ways, marked men. In February 1963 Kwame Nkrumah decided to appoint me Ambassador to Iraq – my first, what one might call, open Government appointment. I was to hold the position together with the post of Editor of *The Spark*. It was decided that Abdul Karim Kassem's régime in Iraq was a suitable one to become the focus of a new initiative in our Middle East policy. He·had corresponded with Nkrumah about the independence struggle and the imperialist tactics in the Middle East, and I was to increase contact with Karim Kassem. I never took up the post because, while I was flying from the Congo where I had been on a short visit, via Lagos and Accra towards Iraq, Kassem was overthrown and killed in the bloody coup of that month. At the same time, as an aside, I was seized by the Nigerian Special Branch while in transit at Lagos Airport. The Englishman who arrested me brushed aside my complaints that I was in transit and said 'You are not suspended in mid-air'. Two white men took me into Lagos to a tower block, and in a closed room with a fire they kept me all that day and the next night, not delivering me back to the airport until the following day. They pulled out a file and read to me in detail the history of my life and then rather pointedly asked me to fill in the missing details, especially in the recent months! I refused to speak, doing no more than pleading my diplomatic immunity, but this was ignored and each refusal was greeted with a slap across the face, or a punch. It was tiring, humiliating and it was very stupid. And it made me very angry. But at the same time it was foolish, conversation being on the lines of (because, although I wear the Nigerian *akbada* a great deal at home, as being the most comfortable and relaxing dress, but on this occasion I was travelling in European clothes)

'Why do you dress like a Nigerian?'

'Why don't you ask me why I am wearing European dress?'

'Why don't you wear that colourful blanket or a bedspread?' (Their phrase for the Ghanaian *Kente*)

'I have a Ghanaian Diplomatic Passport.'

'Absolute nonsense.'

And throughout the whole day and night while they questioned me and searched through my bags, they did not open the one letter which 'S G' Ikoku had given me to post at Lagos Airport. I didn't know what was in it, and it lay there on the table staring at me like an unexploded bomb. Eventually, I was put on the plane to Accra and after I had reported to Nkrumah it was decided that matters would not be taken up through official channels. These were the penalties of the work that we were doing. By our analysis the progressive party in Nigeria in those years was Chief Awolowo's Action Group, and we were close to many of the leaders and of course this was known to the Nigerian Special Branch.

Mr S G Ikoku who was General Secretary of the Action Group is a great friend of mine, and I had also had friendly contacts with Tony Enaharo and Ayo Adebanjo. A number of

Action Group members were attached to the Bureau of African Affairs in Accra. So that there was no doubt that the Federal Government in Nigeria considered that we were supporters of Awolowo's and therefore we were subverting them.

I think that none of us who were involved in these activities in paving the way for independence or revolt against regimes we disapproved of, regrets it or is ashamed of it now. It was in a sense clandestine but not dishonest, so when the military government that overthrew Kwame Nkrumah published a pamphlet giving details of the guerilla training camps we had established in Ghana and in other countries, and details of the arms dumps, the programmes of directions and political infiltration – and when they sent this pamphlet to other governments round the world, we felt betrayed. We had been pursing a Pan-African policy, but it was a Ghanaian policy. To do what the military government did was to wash dirty linen in public, to expose a family argument where it should not be exposed, and to people who should not listen to it. Knocking one's country is the shabbiest and most unforgivable of all faults.

One of the many activities encouraged by the Organization of African Unity was the All-African Union of Journalists and in 1964, I was elected the Secretary General of that organization after the brilliant Malian journalist, Doudou Gaye. We established an international all-African Secretariat in Accra – one of my four Deputy Secretary Generals was the Algerian Minister of Information Mr Ben Belazouk, – and began to gather information and co-ordinate activities in the field of press and all media activities throughout Africa.

The activities of the Pan-African Union of Journalists were approved by the OAU and the UNESCO, but the UNESCO encouraged us to organize the Union of Radio and Television of Africa (URTNA) and the Union of African News Agencies (UANA) and the PANJU under the canopy of Co-ordinating Committee of Inter-African Unions in the field of Mass Communication. (CAMI). The OAU decided to adopt us as one of its specialized agencies. The CAMI was inaugurated in Ghana in 1965 by Dr I K Chinebuah, who was then the Minister of Information in Ghana. A representative of the Secretary General of the OAU was present. I was elected the first Secretary General of the CAMI. This placed a lot of responsibility on me.

This, added to my travelling – for Nkrumah still sent me on missions, to Indonesia for example in 1964 – kept me very busy. I was after all now an MP and I was still Editor of *The Spark*.

By 1965 Kwame Nkrumah often looked and acted like a tired man. The worries and pressures of office were taking their toll and much of the distinctive vigour had gone out of some of his actions. Kwame Nkrumah's involvement in international affairs distracted him from some of the internal problems, both political and economic, inside Ghana. This had always been a danger, but as the economic and political problems grew more serious, the danger grew more pronounced. When, after the Rhodesian declaration of UDI, Nkrumah broke off diplomatic relations with Britain, the economic problems of the country became acute. At the same time the Party was not under control and the bickering and fighting between factions was continuous. Kwame Nkrumah knew what was going on, but he was delaying action on how to control it. He was in touch with some of us and he understood the extent of everything, but the pressures were multiplying. He made that position clear to me during an early morning walk with me around the swimming pool at Flagstaff house. When it was suggested that he should visit Hanoi, in February 1966, I was one of the people who opposed it and I wrote a memorandum saying that this was no time for him to leave the country. But he called me and said that he thought it would do him good, that it would give him time to think about some of the country's problems; he almost saw the trip as a holiday. I argued with him, and with Kwesi Armah, who was one of the main advocates of the trip, but to no avail. I went to his office and argued my case with some of the civil servants. Mr Harry Amonoo, who was one of Kwame Nkrumah's Principal Secretaries, agreed with my stand but he thought preparations had gone too far for any other stand to be taken. The economic worries of the country, the fall of the vital cocoa price on the international market, and the continuing pressures of national and international market politics drove him, to some extent, in on himself. When after the attempt on his life by Corporal Ametewe, he moved one of his offices to the Burma Camp, I thought he made a publicly symbolic gesture as well as providing a clue as to the state of his mind. He claimed and no doubt thought that he was protecting the Presidency, but in a way he was putting himself into the hands of the military, and he was distancing himself from the people – the people who had been his source of strength. Kwame Nkrumah had come to power, and he had retained power, because of the relationship between the vitality and openness he could express at mass political meetings, and because of the emotion he could spark off amongst the people at large when he was face to face with them. The great meetings at the Accra Arena, Subin Valley, Kumasi and Yesuadu Park, Sekondi, became now things of the past, and it seemed as though he had lost the confidence to talk openly to the people.

In my own view, some part of this separation between himself and the people was the result of manoeuvreings by the security agencies. They took advantage of the assassination attempts on his life slowly but surely to separate him from the people. Public meetings became rarer and contact became more difficult. Indeed, J W K Harlley who was the head of the Special Branch, after the Coup said that it was essential for the President's popular support to be removed before any opposition could overthrow him. The crucial gap was thus created on purpose. But Nkrumah led us to the end, despite all the problems, his humanity remained. In 1965, for example, there was a great deal of trouble within the CPP; factions were developing and MPs were not adhering to the party line. At the same time, the press gradually built up a campaign against the behaviour of MPs and their attitudes to agreed policy, and began in a destructive and counter-productive way to run campaigns on the uselessness of Parliament and parliamentarians in general. N A Wellbeck, the General Secretary of the Party, extended the angry debate by saying that the current Parliament had outlived its usefulness and that there should be an election: not a popular view with so many of the members of parliament who were bound to lose their seats. Nkrumah called a meeting of members of the press and members of parliament at The Castle to attempt to resolve the public dispute on ideology. There was a lengthy and prolonged discussion, much of it very learned, on every aspect of ideology and constitutional affairs.

I was uneasy, but I had no idea that the coup was coming. When on the morning of 24th February 1966 I turned on my radio and found the army was in charge; we were awakened by the crash of mortar shells, sporadic bursts of firing from automatic weapons and the roar of army trucks driven hard along the roads; I was as surprised as anybody; I had had no warning at all and had heard no rumours. The radio was calling for senior officials to give themselves up, and in particular was calling for six of us by name, including the Editor of *The Ghanaian Times*, the head of the Ideological Institute, the President's Special Adviser, Geoffrey Bing – and myself. We were being ordered to present ourselves at the Central Police Station in Accra and we were said to be dangerous men! It was, as you see, the ideological members of the Party who were being sought out particularly and in my view this was an ideological coup. The leaders made great play with the economic problems of the country, and a lot of press attention was subsequently given to corruption and rumours of corruption. But it was the political aims of Nkrumah that were attacked; it was his ideological advisers who were particularly sought out, and it was the camps training African Freedom Fighters which were paraded for foreign journalists – like skeletons produced from a family cupboard.

But people remember what was said in public, in the same way that people believe what they are told. At one stage in the three days before I gave myself up, I took a taxi and while I was in it the radio listed again the names of the six 'dangerous' men who were wanted. The taxi driver told me that he knew that Kofi Batsa well and that he was indeed a very dangerous man!

I decided to wait and see if the coup would be a success, and whether the new rulers turned out to have a firm hold on events. So I remained in hiding for three days – two of which were spent in the Russian Embassy. They gave me a room to sleep in and I could relax; but after two days they began to find me an embarrassment, and suggested that I should make arrangements for an escape. In fact, I gave myself up, at the Central Police Station as ordered by the new rulers and suffered along with my fellow detainees a severe beating for my pains. We were all beaten quite badly, before we were taken to Nsawam Prison near Accra – the prison for special and serious offenders. We were joined by three other senior officials who had been captured and there were nine of us in all sent straight to the condemned cells in the highest security prison of the country – with the distinct impression being given to us by our gaolers that we were going to hang sooner rather than later. As we were being assembled soon after arriving at the prison, Kofi Baako, the Minister of Defence, who was one of the new prisoners, insisted on calling the Assistant Director of the Prison to ask him why we were all there and why we were particularly chosen, and what the charges were. He got the only clear reply any of us got: 'If you chop big you shit big'.

There was, and is, no doubt in my mind that the coup of 1966 was ideological. The nine of us who were held together in Nsawam Prison were all political prisoners, and although accusations that were eventually brought against us were ones of financial ill-doing, they were unconvincing. As in the general policy of the new administration, much effort was made to construct a cause for the coup on economic grounds – without concealing the true motivation. The Commission of Inquiry which spent so much time investigating our affairs, found little. They spent some time examaning my affairs and I was totally cleared spending only 15 minutes before the Commission. When I was asked to address the Commission I asked for a Bible and read I, Samuel Chapter 12, verses 3-5. Justice Sowah, the Chairman, asked for a Bible to be sure I was reading the right thing!

But being in prison is not to be recommended even if, as was the case for my first 17 months, there is the companionship of friends and colleagues. In fact this spell in prison I took, psychologically, in a quite light-hearted manner. With the help of Tawia Adamafio and Martin Appiah Danqah I organized a regular church combining the practices of the Presbyterians and the Anglicans; and it was at this time that I really fell in love with the Anglican liturgy. When after 17 months I was released, it was not for long. There was a rumour of an attempted coup to restore Nkrumah and I was put back in jail. I was accused of concealing arms and plotting a coup, of being in touch with Kwame Nkrumah, and of running round the country organising against the military government. Although I had certainly been in touch with Nkrumah in his exile, I had not yet got to the point of smuggling arms into the country. But this time I was put under severe pressure and one month in solitary confinement was a great strain and at times extremely frightening. I was moved from prison to prison, and finally to a special branch cell and questioned and interrogated continuously for four weeks, eventually it was agreed that there was no evidence against me and once more I was released.

CHAPTER TWO

MATURITY

I was a free man, but it was a worrying time and a difficult one to start a career. In Africa, most of the newspapers belong to government and so there was no chance for me to just walk into a newspaper office and apply for a job with a government who regarded me as an opponent, and indeed a threat. I had to start a new career and I decided to become a farmer, as a start.

With a great deal of help from one of my chiefs, Osafoatse Narh Marti, I was allotted 50 acres of land in my home town area, and went into the business of becoming a sugar cane farmer. I was starting with nothing, no money and no experience. I applied to the Agricultural Development Bank, a government body, and because I had the right formal qualifications, the forms were correctly filled in and approved and the money was available for my first 50 acres. By the time the authorities had realized what was happening, the local manager of the Development Bank had explained to me that he had been warned not to extend credit to me, and had said he was going to withdraw facilities, I had been fortunate enough to expand the business to a point where I could stand on my own feet. After a year, I had 150 acres, and the farming business looked profitable. But it was charcoal that gave me a quick boost in the first year when clearing the bush for the sugar cane plantation. I arranged to have charcoal made of the wood that was cleared, put it into sacks and myself took it to Accra three days a week regularly. I sold directly to the retailers (and joined the Charcoal Sellers' Union – my number was 2909), and I estimated that each of these trips brought me a profit of 600 cedis. It was hard work, but as can be seen, it was profitable. It was on one of these trips to Accra that, sitting alone at the Ambassador Hotel drinking beer, I saw an old friend, James Moxon – a former colonial District Commissioner with vast knowledge of public relations and information. When he saw that my car was full of tomatoes and vegetables from my farm, he said, "Come on Kofi, you are too good a journalist to be limiting yourself to selling tomatoes – come and be a bookseller". I explained that I had neither capital nor experience of the business of bookselling but he took me to his small shop, Moxon Paperbacks, and said, 'Take any books and go and sell them and I will give you a commission of 20 per cent'.

That was the start of a new career. I chose some books, put them in my car and took them back to my home town, Odumase Krobo. I took a room and opened a shop, calling it 'Astab' – a name my father had chosen when he opened a bookshop in his retirement. The name was 'Batsa' spelt backwards. I took the books in my old and rather battered Mercedes that I had had for some years and started a policy of taking books direct to schools. Starting in the North of the country, this proved to be a great success. I could get the books to the schools for about 10 per cent of the price and so was clearing 10 per cent on the commission I was getting from James Moxon. The schools, at the same time, did not have to make expensive trips to Accra to collect their needs. Again, hard work and a lot of travelling led to success and, within a year, I was able on my own to go to Accra and open a small single room shop and to make accounts direct with the publishers myself; I was now too big for Moxon to be my supplier. An old friend Julian Rea who had worked in the Ministry of Education whilst I was teaching in Takoradi, was now the representative of Longmans in Africa and did a lot to help me. He gave me good discounts, and he gave me credit, help and advice. He was followed by Amah, an old school teacher, now the Macmillan representative, and Emmanuel Nsiah of Oxford. Within a year my business was as large as any bookshop in Ghana, with the difference that I still took the books people wanted to them, while the old booksellers waited for the customers to come to them.

A natural extension of this business was the move into science equipment. As I travelled to the schools they began to ask me for other things than books, and I realized a whole new line of business was waiting for me. With great help from the firm of Philip Harris International of Birmingham, I expanded into this field. In particular John Haller, Philip Harris' Managing Director, did a lot to help me. He sent an expert to Ghana and instituted a training programme for my staff, taking them back to England and also sending out people to work with us in

Accra. The need in the schools was obvious and very soon led to the next stage: to answer the complaint that the laboratories themselves in which the equipment was used were badly made. So, Astab started its carpentry division which branched out from the maintenance work in schools to maintenance and rehabilitation in private houses and other forms of building.

Astab Books Ltd, for this is the name it came be known, has experimented in other areas of activity, one of these areas in security and sanitary vehicles, but even before my return to politics in 1979 I had decided to retrench our activities a little and concentrate on my first activities of bookselling and farming. At one time as a measure of our activities, the Company's import licences totalled 9 million cedis for a year, but by the time the PNP came to power it shrunk to 500,000 cedis only and, by the time of the coup in 1981 it had dwindled to 125,000 cedis – less than 20 per cent of the salary of my workforce. Therefore accusations that were made sometimes, that political influence led to the granting of import licences, had got things quite the wrong way round. The fact is, it seems, that the bigger you grow, the more enemies you make: or that if you work hard and prosper people think there must be something risky about your success. In fact, working hard is the secret and, my friends and colleagues in my business have, from the very beginning, given enormous support to Astab and its development. J K Twum, who had been in prison with me after the 1966 coup, was a hard working colleague, who began the original Astab bookshop with me. Later on, J K Amusah, who became General Manager and joined the firm when we expanded into science equipment, was a hard working and loyal colleague, as were so many of those in the firm, including my own overworked secretary, Akumatey the accountant, Mr K Acquah, and an old friend, Kwa Asiedu.

I should mention very briefly my attempt to return to the restaurant business. I attempted to start a first-class international restaurant, "Kiko", in Accra with an English manager, and a serious attempt was made to provide something of the highest quality, and it lasted for two years. My illustrious wife, Georgina, put in a lot to make it work but the resources were limited. But it became evident to me that the elements necessary for something of this sort to be successful in Ghana were not and could not be available, and so I closed it. It is one example of my business philosophy which is that I am prepared to cease an operation if it is not working satisfactorily, but at the same time if one sets out in business to make money, it is additionally satisfactory if one also can give a service to society, and can help in that small way in the development of one's country. It was into the service activities that I directed my energies.

I went out of politics and did not play any major part in the formation of political parties after the military handed over power in 1968. I was invited into the National Alliance of Liberals, but I did not join because I felt I could not support their policies and programme. I however gave them my vote at the election.

Professor K A Busia won the election and there were attempts to implicate me in several attempts to overthrow him. It was true that I was involved in the publication of the *Spokesman* which was run by Kofi Badu, but I did not go beyond expressing my disappointment in Busia's administration. I was searched at home and in my offices for weapons which were supposed to have been sent to me by Kwame Nkrumah from Conakry, Guinea.

I thought that Dr Busia carried his anti-Nkrumah fight beyond proportion and he suspected all who had worked with Nkrumah. His overthrow by General I K Acheampong did not mean anything to me because I was not decided on which political line to follow. All through that period I was anxious to succeed in business. I was therefore surprised when General Acheampong sent for me to lead a delegation to meet Colonel Gaddafi in Libya. He said he was told I knew Colonel Gaddafi and he wanted to establish relations with him. I went on the trip and met Colonel Gaddafi. We had useful discussions and I brought letters of friendship to General Acheampong.

When General Akuffo overthrew General Acheampong and decided to hand over power to civilians in 1979, I met a few friends who advised me to throw my weight behind a party which would revive the good works of Kwame Nkrumah.

THE SECOND PHASE OF POLITICS

It is impossible to stifle completely the political life of an entire nation, and throughout the years of military rule in Ghana those concerned with political activity kept in touch, and kept talking. Apart from the normal conversation of everyday life – the thoughts and expressions which no government can prevent – it was common in Accra that any social event of any size; a wedding, or a funeral, for example, became the excuse for the gathering of political colleagues, and an occasion for planning for the future. We, who considered ourselves the successors of Nkrumah, met regularly in this way, and so did the other parties. And so, when political activity became legal again, at the beginning of 1979 – and with only six months left to the General Election, political parties were already half-formed and waiting.

Among the conditions of this resumption of public political life was the condition that no party should have an explicit connection with the parties of the first Republic. The cockerel and 'CPP' – symbols and names being of great importance – were therefore forbidden, and we became, under the guidance of Imoru Egala, the People's National Party, and our symbol the palm tree. As the Akan for palm tree is 'Abe', the joke in the market – not encouraged by any of us – was that ABE stood for Ayeh Kumi, Batsa and Egala – said to be the makers of the new party! I do not think this was the history of the word 'ABE'.

But there were more serious links with the past which were present in everyone's mind, and which contrived to have an effect on Ghanaian politics. The questions were, who were the true successors to Kwame Nkrumah, and what were the policies that represented the true response of Nkrumaism to the problems facing Ghana at the beginning of the 1980s. They were questions which a number of extremist groups attempted to answer to their own exaggerated satisfaction, and they were questions which even came to cause trouble within the People's National Party itself. They were not questions about which I have ever been in any doubt myself.

The phrase, the slogan, that we adopted in the PNP was that we aimed to continue the *good* things of Kwame Nkrumah's government. The emphasis was important, because the view I took, and take, is that not all of the actions of Kwame Nkrumah's governments were admirable, or successful and that however well conceived, there can be little doubt that in practice, especially in the later years, the execution of those general policies was in detail often marred by the distortions of minor political dishonesties. And also it must be remembered that Kwame Nkrumah led governments in Ghana for fifteen years – and in that time he headed, in effect, many governments and developed his policies in a continually changing world context. The application of true Nkrumaism in the 1980s would not have the same priorities or policy instruments as the Nkrumaism of the 1950s or the 1960s. Nkrumaism was the pursuit of economic and social independence, freedom and justice for all Ghanaians and all Africa; and it was based on an objective analysis of the situation with which Kwame Nkrumah found himself faced. Faced with the ravaged and run-down Ghanaian economy of 1979, and faced with a frightened and cynical society, the Nkrumaist priorities must be to take every possible step, as part of an interlocking, methodical strategy, to make the Ghanaian economy strong again, and healthy enough to flourish in the fierce and difficult world of international inflation and slump. The health – in every sense – of the Ghanaian people, and therefore the quality of their lives and the wealth of the society in which they live, must on all occasions be the first priority. And that is the true connection between the CPP and the policy objectives of the PNP.

Dr Ekow Daniels, Kwaku Boateng, Mrs Stella Dontoh and a few lawyers in our group drafted our constitution. It was obvious that all the old faces of the Convention Peoples' Party would jump on the platform of the PNP some of the old politicians were emerging from their shadows and being dusted up. Though it was not easy to stand on the platform with some of those who had denounced Kwame Nkrumah and his Convention Peoples' Party after the 1966 coup, it was necessary to accommodate them but watch and control them. There were new faces which gave us courage. Lawyer Amofa of Koforidua, J B Quashie-Idun, Francis Badjie, Dr de Graft-Johnson and Joe Reindorf were useful new faces.

The most important body in the PNP was the Central Committee, a body which had the direction of the Party in its hands. The timing of the resumption of politics was very tight, and time was against us when we had to begin the procedure of

selecting a Presidential Candidate for the new party. The elections were to be in March and there was to be a General Congress of the PNP in Kumasi in April, so we had two months;
February and March, to make our decisions and to prepare a
candidate to recommend to the General Congress. Some of us
thought the whole procedure, even given the time scale that
was provided, was wrong, but there was little that could be
done about it. The Central Committee met to consider the candidates and to make its recommendation. There were five candidates put forward by various lobbies and sections of the
Party. There was Imoru Egala who in fact was invalidated as a
candidate under the Constitution because, after he had been
Minister of Industries under Kwame Nkrumah, he had been
investigated by the Committee of Inquiry and there had been
adverse findings against him. Such candidates were not
allowed. Moumuni Bawumea could not as it turned out, either
be considered as a candidate, having held office as the Minister
of Local Government under Nkrumah, he was still being investigated and although there were no findings against him – and
eventually there were none – his case was still *sub judice* and it
was held that he could not stand. Dr John Nabila, who later
became Minister of Presidential Affairs, was too young, being
under 40 years of age and thus barred by the Constitutional
rules. Dr Andah, a medical doctor at the Police Hospital, was
an early candidate but soon stood down. Finally, there was Dr
Hilla Limann, the candidate for the North and Upper Regions
Group. When the Central Committee met, Dr Limann was
actually attending the meeting by invitation and we were therefore being called upon to consider him in his very presence, and
it was suggested and agreed that Dr Limann should address the
Committee on his policies. I thought and said that this was
unfair test on anyone – to be asked without warning, to speak
on such a wide range of subject and in such a context. But
Limann spoke, and I thought, and I believe many thought, he
made a poor first impression. He was not an experienced politician; he was not an accomplished speaker; and he did not have
a full grasp of the topics on which he was required to speak. I
spoke out against this candidate. We had adopted a Presidential Constitution, modelled to some extent on the American
pattern, and providing for an Executive President who would

wield great powers and be required to be at the heart of the executive machine of the nation. It was not I said, satisfactory to select a Presidential Candidate at such speed and in this way. The candidate who had spoken had not impressed me, and if the North and Upper Region Group could not present a more convincing candidate, we should adjourn the meeting and look again at the problem. It was essential for the country to be presented with a candidate who would wield, and who could be seen to wield, the great authority that would be his. I spoke for 37 minutes to the Committee and when the vote came it was 17 votes to 1 in favour of Dr Limann! It was an old-fashioned vote, by a show of hands, and although nine members of the Central Committee had come to me before the meeting and said that they supported my point of view, not one voted against the candidate when the time came.

There was a lot of lobbying within the Party for other candidates against the one put forward by the Central Committee in the weeks remaining before the Congress in Kumasi, but none of them made much of an impression. One candidate put forward, for example, was Dr R P Baffour, the distinguished head of the Atomic Energy Commission and some time Vice Chancellor of the University of Science and Technology, Kumasi. I met him twice and talked with him – as I was the one member of the Central Committee who was apparently considering alternatives – and came to the conclusion that it would be a tragic mistake to adopt a candidate like that; it would be a symbolic gamble to choose for President a man who made his decisions according to the chance-swing of a pendulum! And so the Congress was held in Kumasi with only one candidate, and Dr Limann was elected as the PNP's Presidential Candidate, overwhelmingly by 624 votes for him, 21 against him and 21 abstentions. I had made my position clear already, and did not vote. After the vote, Egala said to me 'Limann is your brother: you will support him now.' I gave him my word that I would support the decision of the Congress.

The day after the Central Committee meeting, Imoru Egala called me to see him, and I met him with a few other members of the Central Committee, including among others, Krobo Edusei, A S A Abban and Francis Badjie, who later became the Ghana High Commissioner to the UK. They asked me for my support for Limann's candidature, and said that if I joined his 'ticket' the Vice Presidency was mine. I told them that I had stated my views and that I had no hostility to Hilla Limann. I would wait for the Kumasi Congress's decision. If Limann was elected leader, he would have my full and vigorous support, as a matter of principle. It would not need the Vice Presidency to ensure that.

It was now that the serious politics began, and the campaign proper started. In my capacity of Chairman of the Publicity Committee I called a small informal meeting at Odumase, Manya Krobo to prepare the campaign strategy. We had to move fast and we worked out four main strands, to our strategy:

1. We had a new party, we had a new and unknown leader, and it was essential to give the leader new and fresh ideas that he could present to the electorate. We had to invent and build a public personality which would be quickly recognizable to the country at large, and we had to do this around a man who was straight and simple and not an outgoing personality. It had to be done with policies – and with skill.

2. Our candidate was going to be attacked and so was our general position. It was essential that our slogan should be that we were a party established "to continue the good works of Kwame Nkrumah" – we had to establish a clear distinction in people's minds between the ideals of Nkrumah in the early days of Ghana, and some of the less acceptable and more counter-productive practices his regime was lured into in its later years. We were determined that our image, as well as our practice, should reflect the better things of Nkrumah's legacy and not the worst.

3. The leader. above all, must be seen to be incorruptible. Ghana's past was so littered with confused corruption that what people wanted more than anything was the prospect of a straightforward and honest leader in command of a straightforward and honest nation. In Dr Hilla Limann, we had certainly found our man.

4. The PNP candidates chosen for the election should be as far as possible in the image of a leader, both in terms of the policies they pursued and preferred, and their personal character. They should represent the best of the past but should not be trapped in it.

With the main lines of our campaign decided, I now began to work very closely with our candidate, seeing him every day. I began to get to know Hilla Limann.

Hilla Limann had risen to challenge for the highest position in his country through willpower and hard work. He was the son of a farmer in upper Ghana, and he had worked his way through scholarships and hard work, through school, training college, and finally the University of Paris where he obtained a Doctorate in Political Science and Constitutional Law – at the same time studying History at the University of London. His career had been in the Diplomatic Service and he had served in the Ghana Foreign Office at home and abroad through the 60s and 70s. His knowledge of politics was limited to involvement in local government in his own districts in Upper Ghana and a failed attempt to stand for Parliament in the 1954 Parliamentary elections. He had, because of his scholarly attributes, been asked to take part in the drawing up of the Second Republican Constition in 1967. We had therefore a candidate who was a scholar and a diplomat, not someone who was used to the often fierce battle of politics, and not someone who, by instinct or by years of practice, could bring a crowd to its feet, chanting his name. But he was a man of self-evident honesty, and this after all we had said in our campaign strategy, was essential. He might not move the people, but at least he could convince them that he was his own man and that his very bookishness gave him an understanding of the country's past that could help its future. His loyalty to the country was something born of his studies, not something constructed for the hustings. I remember that when I drafted the PNP's dossier on our candidate and showed it to him, he saw the phrase that he was born in 'a little known village in the Upper Region of Ghana'; this was immediately changed to 'an ancient but now little known village . . .'. The man's loyalties were to his origins as well as to his country. Our loyalties were immediately with him; and our task was to make him the man who people believe could, and when the moment came, would get a democratic Ghana moving again on the road to economic recovery.

Now we built up a small but efficient team to support Hilla Limann in his candidature. Dr Alex Arthur became his secretary, and with him were Dr Ivan Addae-Mensah, who later became General Secretary of the Party and Kwesi Oware, my efficient Deputy Director of publicity. And as we built up our programme, two colleagues were valuable in their criticism of our development. They were Mr Senaa Poku Jantuah, an old politician from Nkrumah's days, who later became the Minister of the Interior, and Dr Kwamena Ocran, who later became Minister of Health. Their comments were always shrewd and we respected their opinions. The role of Dr Ayeh Kumi was also crucial to the campaign. As a Central Committee member, he was most active in producing campaign materials and his enthusiasm affected us all.

We had a party organization; we had a leader; we had a 'father of the party', and we managed to get some funds. We had policies and objectives – and now we had a candidate. In the difficult task of trying to show the Ghanaian people and, to some extent, ourselves, in what way we were Nkrumah's successors and in what way we were not, the most important factor was in the choice of candidates. The constituencies chose the candidate, and the party committees endorsed the constituencies' decisions. But the overall policy was to pick candidates who were fresh and new to politics, who were not just the 'old guard' revived, and not one of the 71 MPs who were elected by PNP voters had been a member of parliament before. This fact is not in itself ideologically significant, but it expresses a determination to break with the past and to give the country a new hope.

Hilla Limann's team travelled continually, and the support of a dedicated and intelligent, hard working team was essential to keep the campaign moving in terms of both organization of the money! Not all of those who joined in the organization of the campaign were as helpful as those I have mentioned. Kojo Botsio, for example, had a talent for engaging in counter-productive activities. He had joined the new PNP very early on, and I suspect wanted to be the leader, or at least to get the Chairman's job. But though he, with Gbedemah, had claims to be the closest to Nkrumah in the early days, he had no loyalty when he failed to get what he wanted, and he drifted away from the centre of the party, becoming lazy and showing considerable lack of interest.

All the Parties really used TV too much during the campaign. One of the reasons the PNP used it was that most of the newspapers were hostile to us. *The Graphic* and *The Ghanaian Times* were not sympathetic to our cause, and we got very little decent coverage from them. They would suppress our stories and create obliquely wounding stories of their own, so we concentrated on television – and engaged Mr Tommy Thompson of the Tommark Advertising Agency for quite a substantial fee (which he did receive despite what he has claimed subsequently) and he worked hard to get into the press and the media, good coverage of PNP developments.

But at the heart of the PNP's success in the election campaign of 1979 was not, I'm afraid to say, personalities or policies; the election was won because we had a large team of very hard workers; we had a large and effective membership who put our arguments, which were sound – in a clear and simple way which appealed to the electorate. And throughout the campaign, at the end of every day, we held an assessment meeting and planned methodically the next stages to take account of reports received from the field. There was no doubt that our candidates turned out to be good; there is no doubt that we were the people's party; we deserved to win because we were well organized and worked hard.

I must mention that the PNP won all the seats in the Adagme speaking area, where I come from, because I put in a lot of work, believing that politics, like charity, begins at home. I had the needed co-operation of Joe Djaba, chief farmer Samadjie and party activists like Sakiker, Nyaunu Borboryo, Ossom Moses Kandey, Liguist Batsa and Dr Victor Narh.

After eight years of military rule, Ghana's situation was desperate. International credit had been suspended, and trade was at a standstill. Nothing was working whether in the commercial sector or in Government. The people were demoralized and brow-beaten by inflation and the fearsome economic and social problems that go with it. The Civil Service was demoralized by the bullying of the military and without motivation, direction, or indeed equipment. When we took over the President's office after the election, there was nothing. All the typewriters had been stolen, for example, and while I went to London to buy essential equipment with party funds, the President's Office borrowed a typewriter from the Ministry of Education. We were starting the machine that had lain idle for a long time, and in reality none of us knew whether we could get it going or not.

While the starting up of the economy and the opening up of lines of international credit were the major and over-riding priorities, there were one or two matters to do with constitutional problems which we now hoped were in the past, which had to be dealt with, and it is worth recording at this stage that the note that I produced during our election campaign on the relationship between the party and the armed forces, was essential to the turn of events later:

The armed forces under the government of the PNP would be shaped and strengthened to stand for the following tenets:

a) to preserve the territorial integrity of Ghana;

b) to assist the police to maintain law and order;

c) to assist the UN and the OAU in their peace-keeping efforts;

d) to assist the Civil Authorities in periods of natural and national disasters.

The economic difficulties which the country as a whole has had to face had compelled the armed forces to operate within limited financial resources. It was our pledge that, like all the other realms of State apparatus, we should resolve the situation and make it possible for our armed forces successfully to execute their traditional roles.

It is the party's intention to bring up the officers and men of the armed forces to such highly professional body of men to courageously fight such situations that are within their traditional role, so as not to be diverted by pressures, both external and internal, to enter into fields where they have no expertise.

The PNP would make all efforts to improve the quality of equipment, the calibre of personnel and like organizations on a planned and long-term basis, so as to improve the morale of the armed forces and enable it to play its proper role as a small, but highly professional, team.

The PNP Government would give every encouragement to the Chief of Defence Staff and his service commanders, to instill in the members of the armed forces a sense of discipline, solidarity and *esprit de corps*, and would not interfere with the institutional arrangements and procedures prevailing in the set up of the armed forces.

One of the major criticisms against the PNP was the way it dealt with the army. Some enlightened people thought the PNP should have had a firmer control over the army. In the army, it was thought that we were planning to destabilize the army.

I think we should know that the central role of the Armed Forces in the political History of Ghana was determined on the day Nkrumah decided to dispense with the services of the British officers seconded to the Ghana Armed Forces in October 1961. This ensured that Ghanaian officers who were not adequately prepared for the positions they were ordered to hold, were not able to deal effectively with the command and administration of the Ghana Armed Forces. Most of them were not expecting the higher responsibilities they were asked to hold. It was only a matter of time before they felt that their high military positions were synonymous with the exercise of political power at the highest levels.

A relatively inexperienced officer corps – pre-1966 – was an easy target for ambitious political opponents of Nkrumah; who were determined to bring him down. The net effect of their subversion was to cause a fundamental change in the position of the Armed Forces in the state. From February 1966, the Ghana Armed Forces became a leading contender for state power. By 1972 this situation had become so entrenched in the politics of Ghana that successive governments, including the military ones, were wary of Armed Forces reaction to government decisions and policies. This was clearly evident during the period of the Busia Administration when the late Lt Gen. A A Afrifa became the most powerful adviser. His power derived from the feeling in the then government that his support was required, if the Armed Forces were to be kept in their place.

The problem of military intervention in Ghana may have been heightened by the system of durbars which was an inheritance from colonial days. The fact that other ranks could be allowed to vent their attitudes on national affairs and the encouragement sometimes given them by their own officers, led to the creation of a highly politicized institution with its own set ideas and quite prepared to go to lengths to enforce them. The coups of 1966, 1972, 1978, could only confirm other ranks' sense of power and it is no wonder that the coups of 1979 and 1981 ensured their active participation.

At the basis of our inability to deal effectively with the problem of military intervention in Ghana from 1966, is the failure of successive governments to decide what to do with soldiers who had held political power in a military administration.

The rapid turnover of officers and men as a result of coups in Ghana meant that we had a large core of relatively inexperienced officers and men who were not able to deal with the myriad problems facing the Ghana Armed Forces and hence the feeling among rank and file that they were not looked after and that their welfare was not adequately catered for. More than anything else this led to the 4 June uprising and may have been one of the reasons why the coup of 31 December 1981 garnered other ranks' support.

With the increasing attraction of coups in the Armed Forces and among all ranks, coups as feasible political options to deal with Ghana's political problems became an acceptable solution. Indeed, among many officers and men with political ambitions, coups became the short-cuts to achieving their aspirations. From 1979, this factor provided the main reason for the attempts to unsettle our democratic experiment and was one of the main causes for the second coming of Rawlings.

The 4 June uprising was the final body blow to the Armed Forces in the sense that it:

a) Separated officers from the other ranks. The officers felt alienated from the other ranks and became insensed at the treatment they received from the other ranks. This lack of trust between officer and other rank was to ensure that the Ghana Armed Forces was divided and the suspicions between the two no doubt created the situation which bedevilled the Armed Forces and the country in December 1981.

b) Broke down the chain of command and authority and destroyed the cohesion of the Armed Forces.

c) Introduced competing ideological interests into the Armed Forces. For an Armed force which was inured on a complete divorce from an interest in politics, this was likely to split the institution. This development heightened divisive ideological claims in an Armed Forces that was already politicized and provided opportunities for politically-motivated officers to intervene.

The 4 June uprising was unlike any other coup that had

taken place in Ghana. For the first time, other ranks, in association with a small group of junior officers, seized power from a military regime that had been in power for seven years.

The Armed Forces Revolutionary Council (AFRC) which was formed on the success of this coup, announced "a moral revolution" and a national house-cleaning exercise. At the same time the AFRC committed itself to holding general elections and a hand-over of power to a popularly elected Government by 1 October 1979. The short duration of AFRC rule and the stupendous task of national house-cleaning it set itself, meant that the Council had to rush through with its revolutionary exercise. In the course of this period, a debate arose within its ranks which was to set the stage for serious security problems, the incoming administration had to deal with between 1979 and 1981. One faction wanted the AFRC to hand over power as scheduled. Another faction which was close to Rawlings argued that given the nature of the problems the AFRC faced and the long term nature of its objectives, the AFRC should not hand over power. In the end, a compromise was struck. It was agreed by Rawlings and the two factions that members of the AFRC and their close associates should not retire but on handing over should go back to their units and hold a watching brief on the activities of the new civilian administration, particularly its commitment to continue the house-cleaning exercise. This was at the root of the subsequent problems the new civilian administration faced; because those who were not retired or resettled, formed a conspiratorial group which was to subvert the civilian administration from 1979 to 1981.

Rawlings himself had the effrontery to announce that he had put the representative government under probation.

It was however recognized by the new administration and the Armed Forces High Command that to remove the threat of destabilization which AFRC members and their associates posed to the success of the new civilian experiment, a comprehensive programme of resettlement courses should be arranged for all those who had taken an active part in the AFRC régime. On the completion of their courses, they were to be retired. This was to be financed by the Ghana Government, the USA, UK, Italy, West Germany and Holland. Unfortunately, because of financial constraints, the programme could not cover all those affected. Moreover, Rawlings who by October 1979 had made it clear that he wanted to come back to power again, persuaded a considerable number of AFRC members and their associates not to accept the offer; for reasons that are closely connected with his intention to seize power in the future. He succeeded because the programme was not compulsory. All those affected were given two options:

1. to continue with their service career, or
2. to accept to be resettled.

Apart from some members and associates who accepted the second option, a significant number of second and third echelon members of the AFRC régime opted for the first option and thus constituted a readily available pool of pro-Rawlings sympathizers, who could be expected to rally to Rawlings when the need arose. They were the people he used in earlier unsuccessful coup attempts between 1979 and 1981 and the successful one in December 1981. Thus the programme had a limited effect but it bought time for the government.

The problems that the post-June 4th Armed Forces posed to the Limann administration were complex. It did not take any serious student of the history of the Ghana Armed Forces to accept that the Armed Forces remained the most credible threat to national stability and the success of the new democratic experiment. An Armed Forces that had mutinied could do so again, especially when the problems that had created the uprising remained and particularly when the mutiny left in its train serious problems that could wreck the new national institutional framework the Third Republican constitution had created. These problems required expert handling and demanded urgent attention, if the new Government was to have the peace of mind to create the conditions for stability which urgent national tasks demanded.

Command had broken down, with the departure and retirement of many experienced senior officers. In many units, command was held by relatively junior offices. Those senior officers who were available were either not acceptable to the ranks, imbued with the post-June 4th fever and their new sense of power; or were unwilling to accept higher responsibility.

There was mistrust as a result of the treatment the senior officers received from the hands of the junior ranks, many officers mistrusted the ranks and were unwilling to have anything to do with them, even on professional matters. The other ranks were afraid that with the departure of the AFRC, officers would come into their own and punish other ranks for their actions during the period of AFRC rule. This lack of trust, despite serious efforts to remove it, persisted right until 31 December 1981.

Discipline was obsolete. The seven years of the military involvement in politics left the Armed Forces ill-equipped. Even when they were, these were obsolete and in a sad state of disrepair. Lack of equipment created morale problems and led to dissatisfaction.

Welfare systems and arrangements that had been devised to cater for the welfare of troops had broken down and in many cases were non-existent.

There had been no serious training between 1972 and 1979. Lack of adequate equipment made this difficult. Because of fears that troops on training exercises might be used for coups, regular and large-scale training had been stopped. It is known that when troops are not kept busy throughout the year on intensive training, they become bored and idle. An idle soldier finds time to indulge in unmilitary activity and soon falls prey to subversive activities.

Politically Ambitious Soldiers who had tasted political power during the AFRC rule felt a sharp sense of loss of authority and were itching to exercise political power once more. A lot of soldiers made significant material gains during 4 June and the departure of the AFRC, reduced their ability to make money and the opportunity to acquire property. They constituted a significant group who were eager to be restored to their former status and could be expected to fall to the blandishments of Rawlings.

As a result of the 4 June uprising, many arms and large quantities of ammunition could not be accounted for. Most of these were held by soldiers in anticipation of the second coming of Rawlings. Others were sold to armed robbers. Still others were held in caches in the Kwabenya area. This was discovered only a few days before the 31 December uprising.

Various options were discussed to deal with these problems.

The first and the most effective one was the disbandment of the Armed Forces, with the assistance of foreign troops. From the beginning this was ruled out by the Government as politically unacceptable. Other options that were approved for action were:

1. To retrain and re-equip the Armed Forces, with the assistance of the British Armed Forces.
2. To sign defence pacts with friendly African and European governments to provide a security umbrella for Ghana.
3. To set up a commission to look into the problems of the Armed Forces and make recommendations to the government.

The first was embarked upon but soon ran into difficulties because the then Army Commander, Brigadier Arnold Quainoo, and some of the officers were opposed to the idea of bringing British training teams to help retrain the Armed Forces. Officers' reaction to the idea was primarily due to the fear that the presence of these foreign experts would reveal their professional incompetence and their general lack of experience and initiative. The Army Commander's attitude was simply based on the fact that he thought it was not necessary to bring in British training teams and that the Ghana Armed Forces could deal with the problem. The result was that the exercise was limited to only service support units. By the middle of 1981, this programme had been largely abandoned. Suffice it to say that the other ranks' reaction was very favourable as it showed them what they could do with new skills. Plans were however made to train fighting units through organized training competitions under the auspices of the British and to organize an UK/Ghana troop exchange in 1982. But this never took off. The failure of the British scheme denied us a wonderful opportunity for entering into close co-operation which would have yielded beneficial results for national security.

The second option was accepted in principle but by December 1981 no such pacts had been signed. Exploratory contacts were made with some foreign countries but the outcome was not encouraging.

The third option was started. The commission was set up under the chairmanship of Mr Justice Charles Coussey of the Appeal Court. The Coussey Commission was initially treated

with suspicion because many soldiers felt it had been established to disband the Armed Forces. Threats were made to dis-
rupt its proceedings when it began sitting. When soldiers later
on found its usefulness, they accepted it with enthusiasm and
called for the speedy despatch of its deliberations. The Commission's preliminary recommendations which were immediately implemented for improved pay and allowances for
all ranks, ensured very wide acceptance of its need and bought
time for the Government. Its final reports were not submitted
to Government before 31 December 1981.

As a result of the election the PNP had an overall majority in
Parliament of one, and we thought that this was not adequate
for comfortable Government. I was therefore empowered by
the National Executive at its meeting at the Legion Hall in
Accra, to undertake negotiations with the Social Democratic
Party and the United National Convention and after much
negotiation, and agreement was signed between the UNC and
the PNP on October 1979.

Dr de Graft Johnson, the Vice President, headed our team at
the meeting, with J B Quashie-Idun, Johnny Hanson, Dr I K
Chenebuah and Joe Reindorf, the Attorney General, among
others, while the UNC was represented by Alhaji Idrissu
Mahama, the Deputy Leader of the Party, R R Amponsah, Joe
Hyde, Peter Adjetey, Dr P Agamah and Dr Obed Asamoah.

The parties mutually declared that the basis of the agreement was 'the over-riding need for stable democratic civilian
politics and the promotion of a healthy economic order and
therefore they decided to form a Political Alliance for co-operation in all matters and at all levels of Party organization.'

We established a national liaison committee comprising
seven PNP and five UNC members for the purpose of consultation. Dr J W de Graft Johnson was the Chairman and Dr Obed
Asamoah was the Secretary. The meetings were held in my
house. The Alliance served for the first year of our administration. It was unfortunate that the UNC unilaterally abnegated
the agreement but did not withdraw their representatives serving in the government.

I must say that the leader of the UNC, Mr William Ofori-
Atta, co-operated with us throughout the period but some of his
followers, like Dr Asamoah and Dr Agamah, joined us in search

of jobs and were disappointed when the jobs were not forthcoming at the rate they expected. Like most of their friends they give the impression that they are fabulous with theories but decidedly short of facts and realities. They have an unreal perception of their fame. I am happy they are trying their luck now.

THE ECONOMIC REALITIES

We set about the task of ruling Ghana. I was interested in all aspects of the economic problems and keenly studied the problems because I was the Chairman of a committee established by the Central Committee of the PNP to oversee the activities of the Ministry of Finance and Economic Planning. The Minister and some bankers were members of the Committee. Experts were co-opted as and when their services were needed. Mr Amoa Awuah, a former Deputy Minister of Finance during the period of Kwame Nkrumah's rule, was an enthusiastic member. Dr Nyakotey, the Deputy Minister of Finance and Economic Planning, gave us his full co-operation.

I must mention that the Armed Forces Revolutionary Council from which we took over the reins of government after a very short term of office – June to September 1979, appeared to have left the scene with an unfinished mission. The return to civilian rule followed an aggregate period of ten years of military rule which had ended in an alarming accumulation of problems of the economic and social infrastructure, and with a national sense of degeneration and hopelessness – as witnessed by the rate of emigration and the accompanying brain drain. Discipline in public financial administration and in general commercial life was at its lowest ebb. We were behind in current payments overseas, and no-one would invest in Ghana.

Thus, in September 1979, the major tasks facing the new civilian government were: to foster a firm sense of political stability and to lay a firm base for the true democratic civilian rule; to seek sure improvement of the financial and economic situation and lay the foundations for the resuscitation of the economy and, finally, to work steadily to regain the good will and support of Ghana's overseas friends and thereby re-establish external lines of credit.

In financial administration, a great deal of discipline must be infused. Utilization of the country's dwindling foreign earnings must be rationalized and the import systems must be streamlined.

The Ministry of Finance and economic Planning held the view that though the Government was watching the overall position of the various areas of the country's political, social and economic life, in the absence of a substantial inflow of external resources to assure adequate inputs for the domestic economy, supplies offered on the domestic market were bound to be inadequate and a steady growth of the economy could not be sustained. The effect of slow to stagnating growth of the economy on the lives of Ghanaians whose expectations were naturally high with the emergence of an orderly and constitutional civilian rule was quite obvious.

The Government was therefore faced with a difficult financial and economic situation, characterized by declining real GDP, high rates of inflation, and restrictive trade and payments system. Over the period there was a considerable decline in world cocoa prices with adverse consequences for the nation's import capacity. Thus, with efforts to contain aggregate demand for the two years, real import levels were low. This had in turn contributed to low levels of investment and declining real GDP per capita. Moreover, the Government's financial position was again under pressure, prices continued to rise at unacceptably high rates, parallel markets were prevalent, and although considerable progress was made, the level of external payment arrears remained high.

The Govenment recognized that the complete correction of the weak economic situation would require extensive measures which would involve a carefully worked out time-table of far-reaching policy changes in the country. It should, in this connection, be appreciated that changes, however healthy and beneficial, which were sudden and drastic in their effects, were not likely to have the political support they really deserved; and the benefits contemplated by the changes might never see the light of day. Ghana's experiences in this respect dictated caution in her adjustment programme.

For medium-term adjustment, the Government decided to adopt a comprehensive one-year financial and economic programme. In support of a short-term adjustment programme, the government requested from the International Monetary Fund a stand-by arrangement for a period of one year, for the amount equivalent to SDR 238.5 million. The Government also submitted separately a request under the Compensatory Financing Facility.

The objectives of the one-year adjustment programme were to stimulate supply, establish viable pricing relationships, increase incomes in the productive sectors, and reduce the budget deficit without upsetting the hard-won internal political stability. In this way, it was expected that the balance of payments would be strengthened, output sharply increased and the unduly high rate of inflation cut back and then lay the basis for a sustained growth of product and exports. Steps were initiated towards the liberalization of imports. Moreover, the policies were expected to lead to an increase in exports. Provided adequate external support became available in 1981/82, the account deficit was projected to increase to $524 million sharply higher than the $104 million estimated in 1980. In addition, the government continued to reduce external payment arrears and maintained the level of gross international reserves, which was needed to assure prompt payment of imports and services. It was envisaged that improved supply situation through increased domestic production as well as imports together with a reduction in the injection of new liquidity should lead to sharp cutback in the inflation rate.

For the realization of policy objectives, the Government realized the need for appropriate formulae to be adopted for a re-distribution to the advantage of liquidity in the system. the export sector of the economy needed impetus by way of increased producer prices for the expected growth of production and export. For contentment and efficiency of labour, the Government realized the need for higher wages and salaries. But there was no doubt that effictive re-distribution of liquidity in the system in favour of increased production and productivity equally required an appropriate tax system which would have the effect of exchange rate adjustment and effective revenue collection.

The Government realized that higher producer prices and high wages have immediate effect because these immediately increase purchasing power and demand. If fresh supplies were not readily forthcoming, prices of existing supplies would immediately rise (especially with a simultaneous implementation of a policy of complete de-control of all prices) and this would ultimately affect cost of production – of labour, for example, through further demands for higher wages. Increased supplies from externally funded industrial and agricultural enterprise might be too late to save the situation because of the 'gestation periods' involved. In a developed, predominantly industrial country, the problem of a gestation period hardly arises because supplies are readily available from local factories. The reverse is the position with a developing country where problems of placement of order, shipment and transport for actual delivery of raw materials/finished goods to locations are real and must be contended with.

It is for these reasons that the Government adopted a timetable for an adjustment programme by which increased supplies to the productive areas of the developing economy precede on a time scale the implementation of declared policies of liberalization, increased wages, and higher producer prices (especially for export commodities which have not *immediate* response for increased output). It is in this respect that external resources for supplies and expansion of local bank credit should take precedence on a time for national adjustment in the economy.

By the end of December 1981, most retail prices reflected the parallel market exchange rate, which was multiple of the official exchange rate of 2.75¢ per US Dollar. This resulted in a depressed export sector which, in turn, reduced our import capacity. It could not be gainsaid that the parallel market rates were a direct reflection of the degree of inadequacy of supplies in the economy. It is true to say that in such a situation, the official exchange rate offers some drag on the levels that parallel market rates would want to take. Accordingly, adjustment of the existing realities without fresh supplies into the system merely created a new set of rates – between the new adjusted rate which became official, and new parallel market rates which emerged to reflect existing inadequacy of supplies in the system.

The view in the Ministry of Finance was that adjustment of

rates *per se* does nothing to improve the supplies situation. Its use must be in mopping up liquidity *in part* from those who require foreign exchange for purchase. Liquidity so mopped up could then be used to promote export enterprise. The volume of liquidity to be mopped up must depend on:

a) availability of foreign exchange resources – and here external resources have a major role in an economy like Ghana's, – and

b) the extent of desireable areas of national activity to be subjected to such an exercise – for care must be taken not to overtax manufacturers for mass consumption.

Adjusted exchange rates also serves as a measure for general realistic price levels in the economy. The Government was committed to the policy of *ultimately* removing all price controls at the ex-factory and wholesale levels. But it held the view that whilst the system of revenue collection was being streamlined, the measures it intended to take in the financial year should aim at a system of excise duties based on the realistic parallel market prices for non-basic commodities. Adjustment in the exchange rate would thus *in part* become a mechanism for a further mop-up of liquidity in the system. All these considerations and measures required careful analysis, selection of areas, and quantification of the volume of revenue expected for purposes outlined above.

The Government recognized that a new impetus must be given to the cocoa sector to increase export earnings and restore economic growth in the long term. Ghana cocoa industry was beset with a host of problems. Low producer price was only one of such problems. Other problems were disease, inadequate inputs, labour, inefficiencies in the administration of the industry, etc, etc. As a first major step, the Government must step up remedial measure already initiated. On the producer price, the Government increased the price.

The Government believed that the higher price would restore a sufficient profit margin to cocoa farmers and therefore would be instrumental in raising recorded output though, in the major part, the reduction in the level of cocoa smuggling during the 1981/82 crop season.

The Government allocated additional resources for improving feeder road networks and purchased transportation equipment, which would facilitate the timely evacuation and export of the cocoa crop. To sustain the recovery in cocoa production, the Government kept developments in the cocoa sector under close review.

Considerable potential existed for the expansion of export earnings from timber and gold in the short and medium term, particularly in the light of the changes envisaged in external policies. Also, the Government planned to improve the railway system and road network so as to reduce transportation bottlenecks and costs. Concerning the gold sector, a preliminary report on the mining potential was submitted to the Government in September 1980, and an international seminar was convened in Accra in January 1981, to promote interest in this sector. Preliminary indications suggested that gold output could be more than doubled within three to five years. The changes in external policies, in conjunction with the new investment code which was approved by Parliament, would attract foreign investors to the gold and other productive sectors.

A World Bank/FAO team studied the timber sector, and its report and recommendations were reviewed for an external technical assistance toward the reactivation of the four state-owned timber companies.

Extensive government price control gave rise to substantial distortions in relative cost-price relationships. Accordingly controlled prices on goods and services within Ghana tended to be much lower than market clearing prices, which had *inter alia* depressed home output and channelled some goods into illegal markets. To correct this situation, the Government had, from the beginning of 1981, initiated moves to remove controls in retail prices. To mitigate the impact of this policy on the poorest segments of the population, special arrangements were made for the distribution of 15 basic goods through co-operatives and commercial houses. The Government was committed to the policy of freezing all prices of control and it pursued the policy with the aim of effecting complete de-control by the end of its first term in office.

For over two years, the Government made a major effort to conserve energy. The Government successfully implemented a rationing system of petroleum sales. Also, retail prices of all petroleum products were adjusted upward on several occasions, and all budgetary subsidies were removed in an effort to align domestic energy prices with those of the world markets. However, retail prices reflected an indirect subsidy through the official exchange rate; but, given the importance of petroleum products for domestic transportation, the Government decided to stick to the formula of leaving local prices to the levels of world market prices. At the end of the financial year, the Ministry of Finance assessed the effects of the package of measures and in turn assessed the extent of the indirect subsidy which existed through the official exchange rate *vis-à-vis* the parallel market rates as obtained at the close of the financial year. Appropriate measures were then taken.

The budget was a major instrument in the adjustment programme to constrain the growth in new liquidity. It, at the same time, provided for high wages and salaries in the public sector, a temporary subsidy on retail petroleum products and allowed a replenishment of supplies, as well as an increase in capital expenditure. In the past, the decline in economic activity and the expansion of unofficial market transacions deeply eroded the tax base, especially with relation to foreign trade. Real public sector wage fell by 85 per cent between 1974 and 1980, and were only marginally increased by tripling of the minimum wage and related salary adjustments in November 1980. The Government believed that a significant increase in wages and salaries was urgently needed to raise living standards, which helped raise morale, decreased absenteeism, and improved the quality of work. In all the 1981/82 budget total expenditure and net lending, including the temporary subsidies, rose to $19.9 billion. Expenditure of this magnitude was accommodated in the programme. With the re-establishment of realistic pricing relationships, the expansion of exports and imports and recovery of economic activity, in conjunction with new revenue measures where necessary, total revenue rose to $17.9 billion in 1983/82. In 1981/82 contained the budget deficit to $2.0 billion. The Government remained committed to taking all necessary measures to this end.

Monetary and credit development were closely monitored to assure that the legitimate credit needed in a reviving economy were met, consistent with the programme's objectives. To this end, total net domestic assets of the banking system were subject to the quarterly limits set out, which took into account seasonal needs and the larger demand for credit in the private sector which was expected to arise. Quarterly limits were set on the net claims on Government of the domestic banking system. Those limits were consistent with the budgetary objectives for 1981/82 set forth above, while providing for a contingency margin. To control total domestic credit expansion and the increase in the monetary base, average cash reserve ratios as well as the ceilings on holdings of other liquid reserve assets to deposits applied by the Bank of Ghana remained in force. In addition, in the light of the financial and economic programme, credit guidelines were revised to permit expanded lending, particularly for exports, imports, domestic manufacturing and agriculture. Moreover, credit developments were monitored much more closely than in the past, in particular by requesting commercial banks to provide prompt information on their loads categorized by sectors. Concerning interest rates, in March 1981, the rate of interest on new Government bonds was raised by six percentage points to 19.5 per cent. Comparable adjustments were made on the deposit and lending rates of commercial banks when revised monetary guidelines supporing 1981/ 82 budget were announced. These adjustments, in conjunction with the envisaged sharp reduction in the inflation rate, enhanced the effectiveness of interest rates in economic management. The Government kept interest rates under close review and was ready to make further modifications as warranted.

Owing to administrative difficulties and shortage of foreign exchange, Ghana incurred substantial current payments arrears as well as arrears on debt service through end-1978. These arrears comprised pre-1972 arrears on import payments; arrears which had arisen on import and service payments since November 1971; arrears with regard to funds accumulated in 1975 and 1976 from sales of equity in conformity with the Investment Policy Decree; arrears from the backlog of transfers of profits and dividends; and arrears on medium-term and long-term debt service payments. At the expense of lower import levels, the Government reduced the outstanding amount of US$165 million during 1979 and 1980, and arrears remained unchanged through April 1981. Moreover, the Government strengthened the co-ordination of the import, with the effect that virtually all new import payments were settled on a current basis. The Government considered it essential for the re-establishment of confidence, particularly in international capital markets, to eliminate the remaining US$350 million in the total amount of arrears. To this end, a schedule of reductions in the total amount of outstanding arrears were established. Over the programme period, the Government also treated each category of arrears in an orderly and non-discriminatory manner, and avoided increases in arrears outstanding in any category. In addition, administrative procedures were further strengthened in order to avoid arrears in the future.

Debt service payments on medium-term and long-term debt were projected to amount to about 5 per cent of export receipts in 1981/82. To prevent total debt services burden from prejudicing Ghana's future growth performance, the Government kept the size and maturity structure of the external public sector debt under constant review, and limited the contracting of official and officially guaranteed debt with an original maturity of 1-12 years to the amount of US$400 million. Within that limit, the Government limited the contracting of such debt with an original maturity of 1-5 years inclusive to the amount of US$150 million. Loans contracted on concessional terms for the consolidation of payments arrears were excluded from the ceilings.

The Government's adjustment programme was designed to realize a major liberation of the trade and payment system during the programme period, in the first instance through the liberalization of the import system. As part of the adjustment programme, the mandatory advance import deposit requirement and export bonus schemes were eliminated. In addition, during the period of the standy-by arrangement, the Government did not introduce any new, or modify existing, restrictions on payment, and transfers for current international transactions, or on imports for balance of payments.

The Limann Administration believed that the policies set forth by the Ministry of Finance and Economic Planning were adequate to achieve the objective of its programme, but was ready to take any further measures that might become appropriate for this purpose. The Government was in the process of consulting with the Fund (IMF) on the adoption of any measures that were appropriate, in accordance with the policies of the Fund.

In the face of all these steps the PNP administration set out with certain basic projects. Dr Hilla Limann inaugurated a Projects Implementation Committee under the chairmanship of Nana Okutwer Bekoe III on 10 June 1981, six sub-committees were established to cover the various sectors in which projects were discussed by the President during his visit to the United Kingdom, Yugoslavia, Rumania and the Federal Republic of Germany in May 1981. I was the Vice-Chairman. The sub-committees were:

a) Agriculture and Lands;
b) Mining and Energy;
c) Forestry and Timber;
d) Roads;
c) Infrastructure (including Tourism, Railways, etc); and
f) The Legal and Finance Sub-Committee.

Apart from its subject terms of reference the Legal and Finance Sub-Committee which was at ministerial and party level (the others being at deputy ministerial level) was to co-ordinate the activities of the other sub-committees and act as a clearing house for their proposals and recommendations before submitting them to the President for consideration.

The Legal and Finance sub-committee was composed of:

Mr Kofi Batsa – Chairman
Mr Joe Reindorf – Attorney General
Dr I K Chinebuah – Minister of Foreign Affairs
Prof George Benneh – Minister of Finance
Mr Opoku Afriyie – Minister of Information
Dr Ivan Addae-Mensah – General Secretary PNP
Dr P A V Ansah – University of Ghana
Mrs A Y Aggrey-Orleans – Secretary

The other sectoral sub-committees held a number of meetings at which they considered the projects which fell within their purview.

The Legal and Finance sub-committee held its first meeting on 19 June 1981, at the Castle, to consider the reports of the sectoral sub-committees. The following were some of the comments and recommendations of the Legal and Finance sub-committee on the projects considered by the sectoral sub-committees:

At the meeting we were informed that the Attorney General had approved the commercial offer relating to delivery conditions for tractors, farm machinery, plant and equipment as required for the establishments of five (5) vegetable farms and three (3) repair and maintenance workshops by the Ministry of Agriculture.

We therefore recommended the President to approve the offer on the basis of the approval of the Attorney General and Minister of Justice.

The Mining and Energy sub-committee observed that Philips Petroleum Company had finished drilling operations in the South Tano area. Philips Petroleum, however, appeared reluctant to drill the North Tano structure which appeared to possess large gas/oil potential on account of earlier engineering difficulties. Philips Petroleum was not particularly interested in gas. It was consequently not making any effort to evaluate the gas potential of the area. The Mining and Energy sub-committee however observed that 'so far efforts by Philips are generally impressive'.

Our committee made the following recommendations:

a) The testing programme for the South Tano area should be expedited;

b) Philips Petroleum should be requested by the Government to drill a well in the North Tano structure and that should be made a condition for granting additional concessions;

c) The Company should also be requested to evaluate the gas potential of the Western Region, particularly in the areas given to the Company.

The Volta River Authority was exploring sources of funding before inviting tenders for civil works and supplies for the Bui project. The EEC, the OPEC Fund, as well as the World Bank, had shown interest in the project and it had been agreed that the OPEC Fund should co-ordinate financing for the project.

The Mining and Energy sub-committee informed us that the VRA had commissioned a study into electrification in each region of the country, which would involve a study of the required extension in the high tension transmission line of voltages going down through 33Kw and 11Kv. The study was being undertaken in consultation and co-operation with the Electricity Corporation of Ghana. The results of the study were expected to be available after three months.

The feasibility study had further been commissioned on the extension of the transmission line from Kumasi on the grid through Brong-Ahafo to Bui and from Bui to Tamale and Bolgatanga.

The Mining and Energy sub-committee recommended that the Western Regional Minister should be asked to expedite action on the implementation of the Western Regional Rural electrification programme. To this end, a letter was issued from the Projects Implementation committee to the Regional Minister for an up-to-date progress report on the project.

The EEC should be approached to expedite action on the studies on the mini and micro hydro-electric project.

Ghana was to decide within three months on the offer of Energoinvest of Yugoslavia to provide part of the credit for the expansion of the Tema Oil Refinery.

The Mining and Energy sub-committee observed that the feasibility study by the consultants, Messrs SNAM Progetti Spa of Italy, for re-vamping the refinery and the bitumen project, gave four months as the period within which the study could be completed.

The sub-committee recommended that the Ministry of Fuel and Power should finalize arrangements and ensure that the Agreement on the feasibility study of the expansion of the refinery and bitumen project was signed as soon as possible. The Profects Implementation committee wrote to the Yugoslavian authorities to accept the offer. The Yugoslav authorities were requested to provide details of the total amount which they were prepared to release and the conditions of the assistance.

An agreement had already been signed with a consortium (Brown & Root) for the studies on the development of Kibi bauxite deposits. The Kibi Bauxite Development Company was formed although finances for the project had not yet been organized.

Ghana was to send a feasibility report on the Nyinahin Bauxite Project to Energoinvest of Yugoslavia by the end of July 1981.

A set of the report which was prepared by the Hungarian firm in 1977 was forwarded to the Yugoslav authorities for study.

The sub-committee on Timber and Forestry recommended to us that Ghana would benefit from a wood-processing complex and proposed that Romania be invited to discuss the possibility of establishing a joint venture company with the Ghana Timber Marketing Board which has two subsidiary companies in Kumasi – Furniture and Joinery Company Ltd, and Ehwia Wood Products Ltd. The following equity shareholding was suggested – GTMB – 40 per cent. Romania – 30 per cent. Public (timber concessionaries) – 30 per cent.

The sub-committee recommended that:

a) a Romanian delegation be invited to Ghana during July 1981, to commence discussions with the Ghana Timber Marketing Board for a possible joint venture to establish a wood-processing complex in Kumasi;

b) the Forestry Commission be requested to play host to the Romanian delegation and to negotiate with them on behalf of the Government.

The Legal and Finance sub-committee endorsed the recommendations of the sub-committee and recommended that the Minister of Lands and Natural Resources invite such a delegation to Ghana. The Ministry should submit proposals for the consideration to the Romanian side together with the invitation; and draw up a suitable programme for the delegation.

The sub-committee on Roads considered that the state of roads in Accra was so poor that action should be initiated as a matter of urgency. It therefore agreed that the Ghana Highway Authority should complete their negotiations with contracting companies and sign the contract for the Accra/Tema roads project by 26 June 1981, after which remedial works could begin by 1 August 1981.

The Legal and Finance sub-committee took note of the fact that the Roads sub-committee had contacted the Accountant General with a view to expediting action on the provision of the cedi backing to enable the Bank of Ghana to remit the sum of £3.57 million, being the down payment for the Navrongo/Mankong Road project.

The Legal and Finance sub-committee took note of the statement of the Roads sub-committee that "the asphalting of the Nsawam/Kumasi road would be undertaken by TAYSEC after completing the 70Km asphalt programme for Accra/Tema".

The Legal and Finance sub-committee therefore endorsed the sub-committee recommendation that AUTOPUT of Yugoslavia could be assigned rehabilitation works on the Kumasi and Sekondi/Takoradi roads.

In its report, the Roads sub-committee stated that the State Construction Company has an asphalt plant which could be quickly rehabilitated and put to work in September 1981. The immediate requirement was for an import licence for $670,000 for spare parts and tipper trucks.

The sub-committee strongly recommended that the SCC be granted the import licence to put its asphalt plant into operation. The Legal and Finance sub-committee endorsed the recommendation of the sub-committee. The Legal and Finance sub-committee also endorsed the recommendation of the Roads sub-committee that to ensure systematic progress the Ghana Highway Authority should provide monthly reports on each project to the Ministry of Works and Housing for submission to the Projects Implementation Committee.

The sub-committee on Infrastructure expressed the view that there was need for complete re-organization of the Ghana Ports Authority. In the light of the discussions which the Minister of Trade, Mr Vincent Bulla, had had with his United Kingdom counterpart on the conditions at the Tema and Takoradi Ports and their agreement in principle that it was necessary to train Ghanaian personnel in ports superintendence duties, the sub-committee recommended that:

a) a formal request be made to the British Government to send experts to help re-organize the Ghana Ports Authority;

b) in the meantime, the Crown Agents in London must be

consulted to indicate the areas in which they could train Ghanaian ports personnel;

c) the Ghana Ports Authority should furnish the committee within two weeks with their organizational chart showing job descriptions and qualifications of their personnel holding key positions.

The Legal and Finance sub-committee observed that an expert was already in Ghana for the purpose of assisting in re-organizing the Ghana Ports Authority and endorsed the recommendation of the sub-committee on Infrastructure.

I must mention that there were a few Ghanaians who were prepared to give a helping hand to get Ghana back on the right road. I must mention the enthusiastic efforts of Mr G. Adali Mortty to get things done. I remember him always saying that we must watch our prices. Prices had to find their levels irrespective of what anyone might preach. In situations of scarcity and rationing, black markets flourish and prices skyrocket. In situations of abundance prices plummet. Rhetoric, threats and appeals should not feature in price determination. I grew used to him and was always ready to listen to him.

Cameron Doud, the journalist showed concern for the Cocoa industry and visited me at home to discuss the problem with me.

One of the developments that I am proudest to be associated with is the Code of Investment introduced by the Limann Government. The state the country had been left in convinced me that a new approach was needed and that the old Investment Code with its inherent suspicion of all foreign motives was inadequate. It seemed to me then, as it seems to me now, that only quick and vigorous action by the Goverment could convince the world that Ghana was a place it was profitable to invest in. I went to London in October 1980 and had many talks with businessmen and financiers. Immediately I returned to Accra I presented a memorandum to the President, in the course of which I said I had taken a very careful look at the proposed Ghana Investment Code and I was forced to express my views on the possibility of the Code meeting the objectives of improving the climate for foreign investment in Ghana.

My opinion was that the Investment Code as first drafted appeared to be essentially a codification of the existing laws affecting investment in Ghana. In that there were anomalies existing in the law affecting investment in Ghana, the Code as drafted did not break any major ground for improving the environment for external investment in Ghana.

It was my firm view that the interim report of the Task Force on Investment (August 1980) successfully examined the difficulties for investment by local and overseas investors in Ghanaian commercial enterprises but unfortunately their recommendations had not been fully observed in the drafting of the Investment Code.

In common with all national economies one should assume that the objectives for the Ghanaian economy must be to provide funds and employment to improve the living standards of its people. This objective had to be balanced with the objectives of risk-taking commercial operations. An improvement in the Ghanaian economy would only be achieved when the environment for local capital investment showed real returns (inflation adjusted). The pre-requisite of this had to be the proper and efficient use of local capital and resources.

To reach this end, efficient, skilled and experienced management and commercial abilities were required. These abilities were being initiated by academic studies at Universities, Technical Colleges, Polytechnics and Business Schools, but a risk-taking investor requires management with experience and integrity. Managers of this calibre would have to show proven track records in organizations of various sizes and activities. We must admit that this necessary management resource was not yet available in Ghana to sustain major foreign investment.

The areas for economic development by Ghana had been identified primarily to meet the foreign exchange shortages of the country and detailed examinations had also been carried out for import susbstitution industries in order to save foreign exchange.

However, it had to be realized that self-sufficiency and a balanced foreign exchange account would take some time to achieve. Western economies which have had many centuries to balance the expectations of their people and the diversification of their income earning operations, are still quickly thrown out of gear by world events and basic commodity shortages. The Western economies seek to counter these problems from a basis of political stability and respected credible management. Political stability is therefore another pre-requisite for foreign investment.

I stated as objectives for foreign investors:

1) The Western economies are based upon responsibilities for the management of risk funds made available by capital markets. In examining commercial ventures, organizations are at all times conscious of safe-guarding their shareholders' funds. This point is basic to management survival. Ghana had therefore to accept terms for investment which initially would appear unsatisfactory and unbalanced to the local national interest. This process of establishing credibility and feasibility for investment had to be the foundation for the growth of independent investment in Ghana. Foreign investors bring not only foreign exchange, meeting the short-term objectives of Ghana, but should provide the school of experience for management and management development. Also, expansion of the middle-class which in Ghana is at present predominantly academic, i.e. doctors, lawyers, accountants, would be expanded significantly to include commercial and technical management. The growth of the middle-class should, following the example of the Western World, bring with it the social and economic advantages which would provide political stability.

2) The initial area of investment by overseas investors would be in those enterprises which showed a quick return on investment, i.e. one to five years. Major projects involving substantial infrastructure and development, although being desireable to the Ghanaian economy, have by their nature a much slower return of capital, i.e. seven to 15 years, and represented in most cases an impossible risk for foreign exchange investment.

3) Another aspect of major projects was that scarce resources of Ghana were channelled into a few projects rather than developing the economy in breadth.

4) As mentioned above, the management of capital is the prime responsibility for overseas organizations. It was my very firm view that it is not attractive for overseas investors to participate in ventures in which they could not control the dispos-

ition of their capital. Majority stakes by the Ghanaian State or local investors in the period to achieve pay back of investment was a clear disincentive to foreign investors. After the capital invested had demonstrated a real pay back, partners appreciating the commercial realities and management requirements for the on-going health of the venture could be found.

5) Foreign investors find their capital in the money market of the world. This capital has to be serviced at interest rates prevailing at any time. Cash flow requirements are therefore such that money is invested by foreign exchange investors, who would have to be assured by dividends to cover these interest service costs. The foreign exchange regulations of Ghana had therefore to be structured so as to secure initially the real value capital invested and also the right for dividend payment in foreign exchange.

The above paragraphs, I was sure, said nothing which was not already known and accepted, but to review succinctly the requirements and mechanism to be coded in Ghana, I suggested the following:

a) The management of the Ghanaian economy
  – certificates for foreign investment securing the right of repayment in foreign exchange of those investments;
  – the right for payment in foreign exchange for dividends, technical know-how – royalties and management services;
  – an efficient and fair basis for the management and distribution of import quotas;
  – a price control policy which would allow a proper return for any particular activity or venture.

  b) An organization of labour resources which would provide for adequate expatriate quotas quickly administered, fairly remunerated and providing a substantial proportion of remittability overseas of expatriates' earnings.
  – provision of facilities, locally and overseas, for the education of Ghanaians for management;
  – improvement of practical skills and the responsible control of our trades unions.

  c) Incentives for the improvement of export performance, e.g. percentage of foreign exchange to be allocated to those companies involved in exports.

d) A taxation system which reflected fair requirements of Ghana's economy, balanced against the attributable after-tax return to the investor.

Selection of Areas Activities available to Overseas Investors:-

– the projects available for overseas investors would be examined overseas on the basis of pay back for investment. I suggested that ventures should be examined on the three bases:

Pay backs of 1 – 5 years
5 – 10 years
10 – 20 years

Regulations concerned with the timing and extent of Ghanaian local participation in these ventures should be differentiated on projects having these different time bases. Further, the tax holdings should also be structured to reflect these three bases of investment returns.

– projects which required a level of technical management, such as medium to sophisticated technology, should initially be available to overseas investors. These ventures would include manufacturing activities and, in some cases, trading activities such as equipment distribution, requiring technical back-up.

I suggested that these activities be included in the ventures available to overseas investors because where they involved foreign exchange, it was absolutely essential from the point of view of the Ghanaian economy, that this investment was not dissipated because of the lack of good management control.

Finally, the benefits of agreement between Government and foreign investors could only be to the mutal advantage of both. It would result in the growth of confidence of international business, which would improve the confidence of financial institutions, international and public corporations and provide the basis for obtaining increasing amounts of finance for foreign exchange for both commercial and national requirements.

I thought we should set up an effective small committee to look at this paper and liberalize the Investment Code profusely.

The President acted quickly, calling a meeting at Peduasi

Lodge at Aburi near Accra to discuss how speedily any action would be taken. The formal policy of the Limann Government was aimed in this direction. My role was that of an advocate who saw the urgency. The meeting was chaired by the Finance Minister and many members of Cabinet – the Minister of Industries; the Attorney General and others, were present and it was agreed that my memorandum, which served as the working paper, would become the basis of policy. I introduced the paper. Later, I was congratulated by Mr Appiah Menka, the President of the Manufacturers' Association, who belonged to the Opposition.

My determination to get the Investment Code enforced as quickly as possibly, and to see it succeed, got me into trouble. I received an invitation to address the Council on Foreign Relations in New York. This was a great honour and one which I could not refuse, and I thought that by the time I made my speech, the Investment Code would have passed through the Parliament in Accra. So, when I spoke forcefully in New York to encourage foreign investors to return to Ghana, there was an outcry amongst the Opposition at home on the grounds that I was not empowered to speak for the Government, and that the Investment Code was not law. When I returned, however, I defended myself, I think well and truly, and as was to be expected, the President was delighted that the new policy was getting known abroad.

Changes in economic policy take time to have an effect and the Limann Government had no chance to implement the Investment Code in 1981. But still remains the framework of a sensible investment policy for Ghana. For the moment, we must just remember some of the words of President Limann when he inaugurated the Code on 11 August 1981:

"The New Investment Code 1981 is the national document that my administration set out to produce so as to meet the challenges and international business requirements of our times and thus pull Ghana out of the stagnant backwaters of modern economic development.

"As you are aware, Ghana had been starved of any meaningful and productive foreign investment long before the Third Republic came into existence. This had resulted mainly from maladministration procedures and callous misuse of national resources, all of which led to the complete loss of confidence in us as a people. The final *coup de grace* fell when Ghana was totally blockaded prior to 24 September 1979 and the trickle inflow of goods for which we were over-prepared to pay completely dried up. It was a very grave situation indeed.

On assuming office, the prime and most urgent responsibility of the People's National Party administration was therefore to quickly undo the blockade, reopen our supply lines, reverse the negative trends of the past, restore confidence in Ghana and create a congenial climate to attract foreign investment.

It was the invitation to address the Council on Foreign Relations in New York in February 1981 that caused me to miss the debate in the Parliament House in Accra. The Council on Foreign Relations is a gathering of powerful and influential people in the United States. I think that talking to this distinguished body was the proudest moment of my life. "Can democracy survive in Ghana?" was the subject they had asked me to speak on, and the Chairman made it clear in the introduction that I was asked because I was one of the few and strongest links between the early days of independent Ghana under Nkrumah and the country's latest experiment in democracy. It is ironical to look back on that day, and on that subject as I write this now in 1984, but what I said then I still believe in and I am still proud to be a link between Ghana's early hopeful days and its troubled later ones.

Ghana, I said, had had damaging experiences in its past and had learned some valuable lessons. We would be offering an open-door policy to investment, both foreign and local, and would aim to make a return to investors of investments in Ghana as attractive as anywhere in Africa. What hit the headlines was the move towards the removal of the necessity of having a Ghana Government majority in any mining investment. Equally important were the moves which I forecast to ensure that foreign exchange was available for the remittance of dividends and that the Government would guarantee that overseas investors could see a return on their capital within a specified number of years. The instability of the past was a thing of the past – that was the main message.

If sophisticated economies in the Western World still felt the effect of changes in the world economic pattern, changes in basic commodity and energy prices, how much more would the economy of small, new countries be affected. But what we were aiming to do, I said, was to build political stability and economic stability hand in hand, and provide an economy; a society which would prove to be a friendly environment for capital. Ghana has the middle-class to provide a social and economic infrastructure second to none in Africa, and it was a society which could, in down-to-earth terms, provide the management that investors wanted. I did not promise any quick solutions. Self-sufficiency and a balanced foreign exchange account would take some time to achieve.

Ghana was now completely committed to popular democratic politics. It was now clear to all Ghanaians that all the military régimes had made Ghana's hopeless situation infinitely worse. Ghanaians knew that the 14 months of the PNP democratic civilian administration had shown, more than the usual 'honeymoon glow', a period of accountability and freedom of speech. There had been no oppression of legitimate protest.

It was true that there were some burdensome portions of the constitution, but President Hilla Limann had never been tempted to tamper with it. We know that freedom is risky but for God's sake we were determined to have it.

We had always called on our people to fight for democracy. 'Crypto revolutionaries' were not unknown in our country, but complacency or, alternatively, impotent rage, were no substitute for dealing firmly with anti-democratic forces.

THE REALITIES OF POLITICS

A number of kind things were said about my talk at the Council of Foreign Relations – and other talks and interviews I gave on that trip to New York. One I particularly cherish was from a young Ghanaian living in the Bronx who wrote to me – I still have the letter – 'It is time Ghana is positively heard again and believe me you did just that. I can only say I am proud of you and sincerely thank you and the Government.' That was a pleasing message, and I think the motives were purer than those of the Opposition speakers who complained after my New York trip that I was the *de facto* President! Another – and ironical – link between early Ghana and the present day arose at the Council on Foreign Relations meeting. William Franklin was in the audience – the first ever black man to be appointed US

Ambassador to Ghana during the last stages of Nkrumah's rule. There had been many popular rumours after the coup of 1966 that Ambassador William Franklin and the Americans were involved in the overthrow of Nkrumah – and Nkrumah himself in his years of exile spoke harshly about Franklin. Franklin was most keen to assure me – both before the meeting and again afterwards, that he was a true friend of Ghana and always had been, and had nothing to do with the events of 1966!

Speaking about the Investment Code was one of the initiatives that I should take – and indeed I had the Code printed myself using Party funds, rather than let it take its course through Government channels. This was one of many occasions the Opposition attacked me and accused me of getting Party and Government matters mixed up. It was a topic that was debated for some time.

The main grounds for these criticisms appeared to be:

1) That Government business must clearly be distinguished from Party affairs. Therefore, if the Government or a Minister was criticized or attacked, any reply must come from the Government itself or the Minister concerned either in the form of an official statement or a press conference.

Where the reply came from an official of the Party who is not a member of the Government, it blurred the distinction that should exist between Government business and Party affairs or interests;

2) Under the Constitution, the executive power of the state was vested in the President and all executive acts were taken in his name. As President, he was accountable to the whole nation and not to the Party only. He had been given ample facilities, e.g. the Ministry of Information and his Chief Press Secretary – for publicising his views, explaining Government action or replying to criticisms only the Government machinery must be used.

3) Under the Constitution, the President was supposed to be independent of every person, institution or group. He could consult or seek the advice of other persons; but save as provided in the Constitution, he was not bound by such advice or other opinion that may be expressed. When therefore a person or a group outside the Government machinery speaks; on behalf of,

or for, the Government was not independent or in control of the situation; or that it was merely carrying out decisions and policies made by persons who were outside the Government machinery.

As against these arguments it might be urged that in a multi-party democracy where groups or parties were engaged in a daily struggle for power, a party could not sit down and allow its Government to be attacked without replying or going to its support. For the fortunes of the Party and its Government in power were in most cases, inextricably bound up together. Whatever discredits the Government undermines its support or popularity, affects the Party also, therefore, when the Government was under attack, the Party must stand up in its defence and help to explain the situation to the nation.

Even though the Ministry of Information and the Office of the Press Secretary were in existence, neither their mode of operation or past performance would suggest that they were inclined to defend the Government, especially where the subject matter concerned the Party as well.

Unlike in the UK or USA, our law provided that no group or association could sponsor a Presidential or Parliamentary candidate or canvas for votes in an election unless it had been registered as a political party.

Having nominated a person and successfully canvassed for his election, it would be odd if the Party could not show a direct and active interest in the performance and activities and fortunes of its sponsored candidate.

Even in places like England and America, where political parties are not given any formal recognition in the Constitution or electoral laws, it is an acceptable practice and commonplace for Party functionaries to reply to attacks on the Government of their Party.

In Ghana itself, there were several precedents of Party officials replying to attacks on the Government. During the Second Republic the General Secretary of the Progress Party often replied to criticisms of the Government or Members or the Cabinet, or even Parliament.

For instance, when Lt Gen. A K Ocran attacked Ministers and Members of Parliament for failing to declare their assets on time, it was the General Secretary of the Progress Party, Mr da Rocha, who replied to the General. It was on that occasion that the Secretary said it would take more than a General Ocran to overthrow the Government. A few months later an obscure Colonel overthrew the Government.

The Limann Administration was commonly referred to as PNP administration. PNP therefore had a positive interest in the failure or success or the administration. Consequently the Party could not sit idly by to watch members of other parties using the precincts of Parliament House to call press conferences to attack the Government.

It should be said that there was nothing in the Constitution or other laws of Ghana which precluded a Party official from issuing a statement to explain or publicize the policies or defend the actions of a Government or the Party.

It might be preferable when only strict Government business was concerned, to rely on the Government machinery only. But where the image, support or fortunes of the Party were involved in the matter at issue, the Party had every right to use its machinery and officers to defend the Government, for in doing so it will be defending itself.

It was therefore obvious that the Opposition forces were determined to drive a wedge between the Government and the Party apparatus, and they were not really as interested in the propriety of Party officials acting on Government matters – a practice which is widespread in many parts of the democratic world today. Also, as some of the departmental Ministers were relatively young and inexperienced men, my attitude was that it was better for me to speak my mind and to take what action I thought I could take effectively, rather than attempt in a roundabout way to put words into their mouths. The Government must seem to be active; and so indeed should the Party.

Another major accusation that was made against me before and after the 31 December 1981 coup, was that I was the *de facto* President, and that President Hilla Limann was a front man for myself and other schemers. In fact, Limann was asked this question in a BBC programme after the coup. It can only be obvious to reasonable men that such accusations can have no foundation in fact and represent no realistic understanding of how politics works. But as such comments were frequent, I feel they must be rebutted. I also feel it is unfair to portray Limann as a light-weight who was being managed by some people.

Above all, it must be remembered that Dr Limann was not my candidate for the leadership of the Party and for the Presidency. I was the only person who voted against him at the Central Committee Meeting which nominated him and I was the one who gave support thereafter to the man overwhelmingly elected by the Party's National Congress as a leader. Similarly, I consider that Dr Limann's attitude to me was one of friendship and respect – but not of closeness, and certainly not one which led him to favour all my opinions.

I would like to give some examples of our divergences – and show that where as President he respected my views, he did not by any means always do as I suggested. He followed the line I proposed in the Investment Code, but I certainly was not doing his thinking for him. And as an example of respected influence on a matter of national importance was when in January 1981 I suggested to the President and the Vice President that an outside tax consultant be attached to the Ministry of Finance.

It was my view that the Government should re-organize the administrative procedures of tax collection in the country with a view to effecting a marked improvement in tax collection. I thought that serious consideration should be given to the recruitment of an experienced Inspector of Taxes from either the United Kingdom or Canada, who have been in charge of tax districts and have had considerable experience in dealing with the tax affairs of multi national companies. He should be attached to the Ministry of Finance and Income Tax for about 18 months to assist in the re-organization of Ghana's tax systems, procedures and effective collection.

I thought it was desirable that such appointments be made from the United Kingdom or Canada because the tax system in Ghana is based on that of the United Kingdom and that in Canada is basically modelled on the UK system – hence, any recommendations that such an appointee may deem to make would not seriously disturb the general system of tax administration in Ghana with which officers of the Central Revenue Department are familiar.

Secondly, an outside person who has served or is serving with the Inland Revenue Department in the UK or Canada would come to Ghana with an open mind and would not be influenced by personalites, as is likely to be the case with the present tax adviser to the Ministry of Finance – a former employee of the Central Revenue Department who resigned.

Furthermore, it would be very useful for the Minister who was not a 'tax man' to have the benefit of the advice and counsel of a neutral but experienced tax administrator.

This suggestion was not followed up. The President took a different line.

The reform of the Cocoa Marketing Board was something that was pressing for long before the subject became a public scandal, and so I quote the memorandum I sent to the President on 1 October 1979:

> It appears no firm decision has been taken on the structure of the proposed Cocoa Council. Owing to the dismissals carried out recently by the AFRC, the morale in the set up is extremely low.
>
> As you aware aware, Ghana obtained 70 percent. of her foreign exchange earnings through the sale of cocoa and this makes it important that a decision be taken before the cocoa season starts on 10 October 1979.
>
> I am, therefore, suggesting that Mr Pianim be invited to a meeting to plan what should be done.

The President took a different line and made his own appointment. A year later, in October 1980, I was urging the President to take forceful action publicly on the financial front. In a memorandum dated 4 October 1981, dealing with the state of the currency, the shortages of essential commodities and the drain on manpower resources, I said the well-wishers of the Limann Administration and Party adherents would wish that the second year just begun would usher in certain visible signs of economic recovery and some relief from the severe economic restraints.

Sure enough, apostles of doom had been prophesying a build-up of ugly discontent which might lead to explosion, the effects of which would be too nasty to contemplate. We could discount some of this gloomy picture which the Jeremiahs in our society had painted, especially those who did so in the hope of partisan advantage. For our part we knew the facts of the situation as they truly were and therefore realized that we dared not rest on our oars until we struck economic *terra firma.* In other words, we hardly required prodding in order to address ourselves to the task confronting us who had gallantly assumed the mantle of responsibility.

At that time my own assessment of the situation actuated me to ask the following questions.

a) What inventive solutions had we thought of which we could share with the expectant public? Some countries were subduing their economic disarray, similar to our own, by thinking up unorthodox measures peculiar to their circumstances. Sri Lanka, Chile, Argentina and India, among others, were examples. Our next-door neighbours, with human and material resources and infrastructures inferior to our own, were pluckily exploiting their peculiar comparative advantage to mitigate their problems. Ivory Coast had her difficulties, but the country had chalked an annual growth rate of two percent or better.

Those who were privileged to know the courageous explorations which the government was making to capture international confidence and respectability, and the anxious thinking which was under administration's efforts to ease the burden on Ghanaians had not two minds about how commendable the efforts were.

We should share information about these efforts, these jobs in progress. We should unleash the potentialities for public participation and enthusiasm of which our countrymen were capable. Voluntary contributions like those of the workers of P & T could be summoned, beginning with ward initiatives and community self-improvement. Imagine what Accra or Sekondi would turn up to be given the spur to offer spontaneous city clean-up and renovation. The roads, so deplorable – especially in the cities – could do with voluntary labour at weekends. Contractors would rally with vans and chippings, given the bitumen and technical direction by Ghana Highway Authority, SCC, PWD, and city engineers, if any. Should we try out a campaign code-named: *Community Action?*

b) The status of the cedi had systematically worsened. A policy of tight money supply and prudent application of financial regulations could hurt. Reduction of redundant labour was politically forbidding. But, people were hoping some way could be found to build respectability for our currency. I thought we must find a way of challenging the Ghanaian brain pool. In line with this thinking, I constantly consulted G Adali Mortty, whose views on national issues were clear and non-partisan. He was prepared to go to any lengths to help ease the situation.

c) Inaccessibility of supplies of commodities continued to bother the nation. Dependable system of distribution had continued to elude us. The current system was fraught with danger. It was based upon a false promise, namely, that certain regional, district and ward representatives could withstand the temptation of handling supplies which were in short supply. Experience of our recent past experiments should have been the guide.

d) Outflow of manpower was depleting our human resources at an alarming rate. We might not be able to halt the exodus. But, at least, we should monitor the rate of outflow, and should have the statistics. Were we trying to keep track of the drain? Meanwhile, the situation was analogous to pouring water in a basket, while we spend on education at one end, and the end result exists at the other.

A year later I wrote another letter to the President, setting out my concerns about the state of the Government and of the country, and urging action to redress the situation over the Cocoa Marketing Board scandal, and the faltering IMF negotiations. The letter is too long to produce in full, but the general drift of my argument was that I had been gravely disturbed by the mood of the country at that time. There appeared to be a pervasive feeling of despondency which could only give cause for real concern.

Even without access to official data, one could see all too clearly that the economy was in very bad shape. The export sector was evidently near collapse. The scandal in the cocoa industry only served to highlight the steeply declining earnings of what was once the world's largest cocoa-producing nation. Timber had ceased to be the major foreign exchange earner it was, and we could visualize tragic declines in gold, diamonds and other minerals.

At home, prices had assumed dangerous dimensions. Some

might speak of prices finding their levels, but the truth was that these levels were intolerable to the people and to pretend otherwise was to risk possible explosion.

In my view, a change of style or direction was called for, and the second anniversary of the Third Republic seemed to me the appropriate occasion to bring this about.

A change of style was necessary because what was conceived as a methodical, sober approach to government was giving people the impression that the government was rudderless and merely drifting. A change of direction too was necessary because it seemed obvious that unless certain tough measures were taken now, the immediate future could hardly be guaranteed.

I was aware of the tragic circumstances in which the government had had to operate. Given the dangerous situation at the time of its assumption of office, the Government could not be expected to take any drastic measures which could upset the security of the nation. Having been compelled to devote all efforts towards creating a stable environment, the Government now found that time was running out for any tough measures.

Even so, I believed that the situation offered a challenge for some courageous action to rekindle public confidence. In my view, the anniversary should be used to send the signal that a new, tough, imaginative and vigorous administration was taking charge. The signal should include a move to have the office of the President take hold of economic policy and the direction of the instruments of propaganda and persuasion, but it should not fail to bring out the long knife in dealing with the machinery of Government.

I thought the time had come for Government to accept the need to reduce the budgetary deficit through drastic cuts in expenditure.

A ban on subsidies to all un-productive state enterprise would seem to be a good starting point and a study might be immediately undertaken into the possibility of converting the National Reconstruction Corp's farms into self-supporting co-operative farms.

A major shake-up of the administration seemed called for. I believed that people generally wanted to see a strengthened Office of the President with the Presidency seen to be directing the ship of state in a more visible sense. I was forced to give a warning in *The Punch* of 7 September 1981 when I told the Editor, Mr Prince Godwin that "I see a train coming, carrying late and undue vengeance. If you open your ears, you will hear the whistle"

I tried on some occasions to draw the attention of the President to the international situation *vis-à-vis* the Ghana situation. I held the strong view that Ghana must seek a diplomatic alliance with Nigeria. I told the President and later on had a long discussion with Dr Wayas, President of the Nigeria Senate on the subject. I told them that after the electoral landslide in favour of Ronald Reagan, a conservative, it was my view that it seemed to re-inforce what political observers had seen to be a current world trend towards the right. The conjectures for a White House outlook on Africa as a whole, and hot spots such as Namibia, Mozambique, Zimbabwe, the Horn of Africa, the spluttering explosion of hostilities in the Gulf between Iraq and Iran, the convulsions in the Middle East, North Africa and across the East African States, not excluding hitherto uneventful Kenya and Tanzania: it was anybody's guess what the period portended for Africa and the world.

If one threw oil politics on to the unstable world situation, then the convulsions in the major sources of world oil must loom rather ominous indeed.

How would President Reagan react to these situations? With allegations regarding Gadaffi and the force of destabilization at work in the Chad, the Gambia, Senegal and elsewhere, how would the non-oil states of the continent shape up in the unfolding threatening scenario?

In the scheme of things, neither President Ronald Reagan of the United States of America, Mrs Thatcher of Great Britain, nor the Chancellor of the Federal Republic of Germany, could brush Nigeria aside. Both in oil and trade potential, Nigeria commanded a hearing of the conclave of world geo-politics.

The indications for foreign policy for Ghana seemed to be clearly discernible. We must strengthen the hands of Nigeria to exert the necessary influence wherever the affairs of the African States, especially those still under alien domination, were discussed and decided. Indeed, our own national interests dictated the need for close alliance with Nigeria.

The question always came up: How exactly should we proceed to forge a strong alliance with this our next-door neighbour? Fortunately, President Limann's sensitive appraisal of the diplomatic requirements towards Nigeria had made him visit Nigeria upon his assumption of office as President and Head of State. I accompanied him to Nigeria where he performed very well at an open press conference.

I therefore suggested that the following measures and steps should be considered: deliberate approaches should be made to bring Dr Limann and President Shagari closer. We should suggest to Nigeria to take initiative to link up and concert their oil strategy with Mexico and Venezuela, the three of which states produce some eight billion barrels of crude as against the nine billion barrels produced by the Gulf Oil States. Ghana's consultations might strengthen Nigeria's hand to seal up their own Three-Nation OPEC power which America could not ignore.

Ghana should diversify its sources of oil supply by negotiating a 180-day credit facility with Mexico and possibly Venezuela. The gathering inter-African events would appear to indicate cautious reliance on Libyan oil.

Dr Limann took the initiative and the issue was developed for discussion. He did not do it exactly as I suggested. He took his own line of approach and visited Nigeria with Dr K Chenebuah, the Minister of Foreign Affairs. Mr Imoru Egala and others made regular visits to Nigeria and I kept my close relations with Dr Wayas and later had meetings with President Shagari.

These examples are given to show that Dr Limann and I did not always agree on every issue. I did not have a regular and close influence on the detailed policies of his government. I have been asked why I did not become a Cabinet Member. The answer is implied by these memoranda and letters. I wanted to lead my own life as a businessman and give way to the new generation of politicians. But at the same time I felt I could and should put forward my views on the main subjects of the day, representing the role of the Party, and give the Party and the Government what time I could spare and what suggesions my political experience led me to. How effective I was could only be measured by Dr Limann's own answers to a BBC question to him about me on 19 March 1982, three months after the coup which overthrew him. He said: 'You mentioned Kofi Batsa. He was anxious to work. This is what I know about him. If there was anything to be done, he was always ready whether it was daytime or night. He worked.'

He told President Sekou Touré of Guinea in my presence that I played a major role in the victory of the PNP at the General Election.

Two of the most important activities I was engaged in in my publicity role came together in a trip to the United States with Kofi Badu in August and September 1980. The need to build up the image of our President, together with that of his Government went, in my view, hand in hand with the need to persuade investors throughout the world that Ghana was now not only democratic but stable. It was essential therefore that the USA, the most powerful nation in the world, had a positive and informed image of Ghana.

An encouraging start was with the *New York Times*, which had earlier taken an extremely hostile view of Ghana and its future, and which after our visit published two articles based on an interview with President Limann, which were approving and positive. We managed to make some progress with this paper and with others, and in Washington, with the important task of opening up lines of communication with the American Government and media; but the most important initiative was through contacting Mr Haskell Ward who was one of the Georgian young men who worked closely with President Carter. He was the Deputy Mayor of New York. He gave us very useful advice on the ways to establish a regular and effective 'Ghana Lobby' in the US, and on the two crucial economic and financial questions that were concerning us – the renegotiation of the VALCO agreement and the IMF attitude for aid to Ghana, would take time, and all would depend on the America perceptions of the stability and determination of the new Government.

The problem of the VALCO agreement was more precise and more delicate. President Nkrumah's Government had signed an agreement with the vast Kaiser Corporation for the building of the Volta Dam and for the terms on which Kaiser would take the resulting electricity and use it for its aluminium smelter. Over the years the changing prices of world energy had made this agreement increasingly uneconomic from Ghana's point of view. Kaiser was permitted to buy power from Ghana at a far lower rate. It was obvious from an economic point of view and from the public and political point of view inside Ghana that it was necessary to renegotiate the contract with Kaiser. At the same time there was no legal need for the Kaiser Corporation to ameliorate its terms and excessive and public pressure for them to do so might well affect our attempts to build American confidence in Ghana.

Americans had been impressed on our trip, by the fact that it was people with what one might call left-wing pasts, who were putting to them with conviction the new rational policies being applied to Ghana's economic affairs. It would be confirming the worst fears of the American establishment if we plunged in too loud and too fast, to attempt to force the Americans to re-negotiate a perfectly valid contract. It was not the atmosphere in which new investors would want to come to Ghana. Haskell Ward was invaluable in advising us on the American attitude on these matters and in a visit which he paid to Ghana in the next month, October, he gave the President a sympathetic account of America's view of Ghana's attempts to right its economic situation. President Limann, on my suggestion, concentrated on three general themes:

1. That Ghana was totally committed now to democratic institutions and needed support from countries which approved of us.

2. That Ghana was an ideal candidate to play the role of an economically successful democracy in Africa, and a friend to the democratic world.

3. That the USA should use its influence to moderate the terms on which the international aid agencies would offer aid to Ghana.

More precisely, there came out of these discussions – both in New York and Accra – first very tentative and highly confidential move towards a renegotiation of the VALCO agreement. Neither side wanted to create a political storm which would injure both parties, and it was agreed that a preliminary discussion should take place with the American Ambassador to Ghana, and I make a note of the substance of my discussion with the American Ambassador just after my visit to America and Mr Haskell Ward's visit to Ghana.

One of the major trips I took during the period of Limann's administration was a visit to Guinea, as the leader of a Ghanaian delegation. It was in November 1979. I met President Sékou Touré after so many years. He received me warmly and drove me in his personal car through Conakry to a villa which he told me was where Kwame Nkrumah had lived.

On the second day, President Touré organized a reception for us and I was very happy to meet some old friends of mine – Diallo Saifoulaye, who was very pale (he died a few months after I left Conakry), Ismael Touré and Diallo Aboudulaye. There were others I missed but I thought I should not ask of them.

On the third day, there was a parade of the military and the youth to commemorate the defeat of the Portuguese invasion three years back. Early in the morning, President Touré himself drove me to the parade. To my utter surprise, he asked me to stand in an open car with him through the streets of Conakry and then to the parade ground. The crowd yelled and cheered as we approached the centre of the ground. I was overwhelmed by the way the crowd received us. Sekou turned to me and said 'Kofi, do you know you deserve this'. This statement rang through my ears for weeks.

On the fourth day I had a long discussion with him which touched on Kwame Nkrumah, Jerry Rawlings and Limann. He suggested that Limann should give some assignments to Rawlings to keep him busy. He thought he had got something which could be used. He got that impression in Havana, Cuba, when he met him. He repeated this suggestion when I met him again with Limann and Nana Okutwer Bekwei III. But it was obvious to us that Rawlings was not prepared to work with us. He wanted to be his own boss. He has got a hunger for power in its naked form, not to improve the lives of others, but to manipulate and dominate them, to bend them to his will. His hunger is so fierce and consuming than no consideration of morality or ethics, no cost to himself – or to anyone else – could stand before it. The flunkeys who hold him out not just as a consummate politician but also as an immaculate human being, have long since been made to look ridiculous. By practice and habit he is a stranger to the truth, he suffers from the additional liability of being simultaneously both vain and vulgar.

Sekou later discussed the economic situation with us. I told him we met an empty chest but the people have not got the patience to wait. He immediately offered us 200 cattle to be delivered before Christmas. Unfortunately, the bureaucracy of the government system delayed the supply.

President Touré met me again on the night of our departure and kept on stressing that though he was happy we were determined to follow the teachings of Kwame Nkrumah, we should by all means avoid some of his mistakes. He repeated this when I met him again in the company of President Limann and Nana Okutwer Bekwei.

Two months later I had the rare opportunity of meeting an old stalwart of the Pan-African movement, Dr Dosumo Johnson who was the adviser on African Affairs to the late President Tubman of Liberia. We attended most of the early Pan-African meetings together. He appeared to be in the autumn of his life. To my surprise he repeated what Sekou Touré told me – three times.

THE REALITIES OF GHANA POLITICS

I will give an example of the way in which actions of mine, and of the Limann Government, were deliberately misinterpreted by the Opposition press. I have described the economic situation of Ghana when President Limann came to power, and the lack of any form of foreign exchange, or investment potential is common knowledge. There had, for example, been no new text books in the country for several years, and the large printing works at Tema had run down for lack of work and the result of paper shortages. When President Limann visited London in 1981 one of the people he met was Harold Macmillan, Chairman of his own publishing firm, which had in the past published many books for Ghana. It was agreed in consultation with directors of Macmillan that the firm would give a large loan to Ghana, on very advantageous terms, for the supply of text books for schools and separately for the refurbishment of the Tema printing works. We saw this then as I see it now, as an obvious example of encouraging foreign capital to invest in

Ghana on the best possible terms to provide commodities that were urgently needed by the Ghanaian people. The press, however, picked up the story in the most critical way possible, and said not only was the Government handing over the text book industry and our children's education to a foreign firm, but it was all my doing!

In fact, when President Limann returned from the UK, meetings were held at Ministerial level: meetings of at least 18 people, including the Minister of Education, the Minister of Information, The Attorney General and many senior civil servants, to discuss the proposals put forward by Macmillan. I attended only some of these meetings and yet after proposals had been put forward in Cabinet, and letters of intent had been signed by the British firm, it was still assumed that I was the person who had arranged it all. Very flattering, but scarcely realistic. What makes it apparent that the interpretations put on this arrangement by the press were totally untrue, was the fact that similar arrangements were either made, or about to be made, with other firms. Naturally, when they heard that Macmillan were entering into a major arrangements for supply of books, the firm of Longmans felt their position might be threatened and, after high level negotiations, they offered a loan of £1 million on similar 'soft' terms to Ghana. This arrangement had been accepted by the Government before the coup, and at that stage, December 1981, the firm of Penguin, a subsidiary of Longmans, had offered another loan totalling £½ million. So, as Macmillan pointed out when they came out with a public statement, the terms of the contract were correctly and openly arrived at; and in additon to that, they were not unique and there was no monopoly involved. In an atmosphere of allegations of corruption, corruption was assumed to be everywhere.

It seemed to be assumed very often by the Opposition papers and by the spokesman put forward by Rawlings in 1980-81, that I had a very large degree of control over the press in Ghana. (There is even some suggestion in the Rawlings-inspired statement from Accra, that I still controlled the press in Ghana in 1982, from abroad!) Now, during the years of the Limann Government, I was a member of the Press Commisson, but members of that Commission will agree that I was not a regular attendant of meetings – there again, critics would no doubt say that although I was abroad when a decision was made, or when a journalist was sacked from his post on a newspaper, that I had somehow arranged it when I was on my travels. Apart from anything else, to suggest that I could influence the Press Commission in these ways, would be an insult to the Chairman, Kofi Badu, who had his own mind and his own policies. I certainly admit that, as the Chairman of Publicity for the Press I had and have many good friends in the press.

Christian Aggrey, the editor of the *Ghanaian Times* was for example, a very good friend of mine, and we often discussed politics and the affairs of the country. I am sure he will admit today that I would very often try to resist when he would attempt to discover from me what the Government's policy or intentions were. There were occasions, many occasions, when I could not reveal what I knew. I had to preserve the discretion that my role in the administration required. As Chairman of the Party Publicity Committee, my job as I saw it was to explain the objectives and the policies of the Party to anyone and everyone – and especially to build the Presidency. Democracy had been restored to Ghana; we had a new Party and a new Government, and we had a President who had never held office before. In this situation it is the duty of someone whose job is basically that of public relations for his Party, to use every means and all powers of persuasion to explain the policies of his leader and of his party to the world at large. That objective explains my relationship with the newspapers; persuasion I will admit to, gladly and indeed proudly; undue influence, or improper influence, I do not.

I regarded my job as promoting, protecting and serving the Government in practice. There was an incident which has other lessons as well. A few months after the Limann administration took office, I was at the Ghana Club when the Vice President, Dr J W de Graft Johnson, rang me and called me urgently to come to The Castle. There was a distinguished gathering of people in the Vice President's office. Apart from the Vice President himself, there was the Minister for Presidential Affairs, Dr Nabilla; the Minister of Defence, Mr Raley-Poku; the Head of Special Branch; the Head of Internal Intelligence and others. They were all worried and agitated because the news had come through that a group of army officers who had earlier been imprisoned by the AFRC had escaped from jail. There was no clear explanation how they had managed to escape, what their motives were or where they had gone to. If this event might be a coup in the making or it might be a pure escape, nobody knew.

The Director of Prisons was called, but he had no clear explanations of the events of the day, or of his security arrangements, and incidentally when he said that the keys of the prison were still there, I suggested he should go back to collect the keys. The Inspector-General of Police could give no information on the escaped men and we decided that the most important thing to do was to broadcast to the country and give the population the full facts and warn them of the possible outcome. When those of us who had decided to go to the broadcasting station arrived there, the policeman on duty at the gate was asleep, covered in cloth against the mosquitoes. the TV studios were open and unprotected, and when we left after the broadcast was called off, the single man on duty was still asleep. I told my colleagues that, 'Except the Lord keepeth the city, the watchman waketh in vain.'

It was obviously important to get to know the position of Flight Lieutenant Rawlings and so he came to our meeting with Dr Limann to make a statement supporting the Government's position and denying complicity with the escaped officers. Rawlings was anxious to issue a statement; the first comment he made himself spontaneously was 'the boys who did this were cowards'. But when, in the presence of Brigadier Nunoo Mensah who joined us later, I went through the draft statement with him, I asked Rawlings whether he wanted to confirm his loyalty to the Government or the State – which word would he like to use. 'Anything will do', he said. There seemed to be no doubt to me about the priority of the situation, and indeed my first responsibility was to protect the Government, so I inserted the word 'Government' in the statement. Brigadier Nunno Mensah suggested that it should be loyalty to the State but Rawlings was unconcerned, was very friendly, he even urged me after the meeting to keep in touch with him and with his Aide, Captain Tsikita, who, according to him, held me in high esteem. He apologized to me for an earlier statement he had made indicating that I was leading a press campaign against him.

A few weeks after the meeting, Rawlings went to a rally in Takoradi and in a comment on the statement he accused me of having deceived him and tricked him – in a matter which seemed and still seems to me to be a straightforward matter of loyalty, and which at the time appeared to be of no consequence to him.

There were many accusations of corruption made during the course of the Limann administration. I cannot answer for all of them and I certainly cannot say that all of the Party was pure, or that there was no corruption in any part of the Government and its administration and the country at large. All I can do is comment on some of the accusations that affected me, and perhaps the reader can draw conclusions as to whether some of the other accusations that were made had the same lack of foundation.

In one case, a story was put about by some of the Opposition politicians that I had been involved improperly in a contract being arranged between the De La Rue Company in London and the Bank of Ghana – the sum involved being rumoured to be £2.7 million. The story circulated widely, and caused a lot of damage to the Government's reputation and to me.

The De La Rue Company issued a statement denying that there was any truth in the rumour and, indeed, there certainly was no truth in the story. the Bank of Ghana stood firm by the fact that I had no knowledge of or connection with the printing of currency notes for Ghana. In fact, immediately the allegation was made by 'Free Press' the Bank of Ghana reacted. The Deputy Governor, Y M Sarpong, made a verbal report on the award of the contract for the printing of Ghana currency to Messrs Thomas De La Rue & Co Ltd to Professor George Benneh, the Minister of Finance and Economic Planning.

In a letter which followed, Mr Alex Ashiabor, the Governor, explained to the Minister that when the tenders from Messrs Bradbury Wilkinson & Con and Messrs Thomas De La Rue were considered by the Board of Directors of the Central Bank at their meetings on the 25 and 29 September 1981, it was found that Bradbury Wilkinson & Co had quoted a price of £19,420,840, based on an index of 321 but their quotation would vary with a movement on the index. As at the 29 September 1981, when the tender was before the Board, the index had risen to 358 which meant an automatic increase of 11½ percent in their quotation. Their quotation as at 29 September 1981 had consequently moved from £19,420,840, to £21,654,238. Going by the historical movements in the index over a period of one year, the total amount payable under their quotation would be £24,685,829.

Thomas De La Rue, on the other hand, quoted a fixed (nonvariable) figure of £22,430,280 which, they stated, was subject to further negotiation with the Bank. Taking advantage of the offer of further negotiation on the price, the Bank met representatives of Messrs Thomas De La Rue & Co, and secured a discount of 1.7 percent amounting to £388,022. The final price agreed with Thomas De La Rue who won the tender was therefore a fixed sum of £22,042,258. From the foregoing facts it was obvious that the allegations in the newspapers by Odoi-Sykes, a member of Parliament who was noted for his clumsiness in politics, were baseless and mischievous. Too much politics was made of the allegation and people who should have known better were involved in this dirty political mudslinging. In fact cynicism was in abundance and hell itself was let loose on me.

The publisher of the *Free Press* took everything on his shoulders with unmerciful ferocity and raised the issue to an unbelievable height of folly. He let loose his newspaper which turned coarse and demented during that period on me. He was determined to seek revenge for his friend who lost the contract. He forgot that when one is going to take revenge, he must look for two graves – one for himself and one for his enemy. I am sure somebody is now lying in one of the graves.

I was surprised when I read a statement on the issue signed by Colonel Frank Bernasko, Leader of the Action Congress Party. It read like a cliché of a picture type of fiction. I always held him in high esteem and thought he did not believe in a short route to political power. Before that statement he sounded to me like somebody who knew that to get to solid political power one must build his position brick by brick and carefully construct an edifice.

I have always maintained that the vast personal fortune I was said to have made was a myth – a newspaper fortune which was so secret that I even was unaware of its whereabouts.

I am sure it is a mystery that the press up to date has not been able to solve.

Perhaps I was a target for these accusations of corruption as much as any because I was both a successful businessman and was now in a position of power in the PNP. In the atmosphere which unfortunately developed in 1980-81, in which corruption was assumed to be rife, it was naturally assumed that someone in my position was corrupt. And I was, it must be remembered, Chairman of the Ghana Industrial Holdings Corporation, which was the largest industrial organization in Black Africa. If he has all this power and all this money at his command, people said, he must be corrupt. In fact, my view was that these jobs – my chairmanship of the Ghana Industrial Holdings Corporation and my roles on the Ghana Press Commission and the National Development Commission – were all part-time jobs, and that for part-time jobs, one should not be paid. So I refused to draw my allowances and expenses for these positions, and had in fact refused to accept cheques when they were brought to me – this paradoxically was not to my advantage, as the rumour seemed to go round that I had no need of these small benefits when I had my hands on so much greater ones! A friend in fact came to see me on 28 December 1981 – three days before Rawlings' coup – to urge me, I remember, to accept my allowances because people were misunderstanding the gesture. It was, of course, only a small gesture – but at least I thought I could make some sort of symbolic sacrifice.

I had been a businessman before I re-entered politics and I had my savings and my investments, my houses and my cars. Now that I was active in politics again, I paid less attention to my business, which in fact declined in the way I have described, during the years 1979-81, but I still had enough to live on, indeed was comfortably well off – and had no need of additional income from Government or any other source. When the Limann Government came to power, the value of the import licences allocated dropped by 64 per cent, and in my role as a businessman I complained to Mr F K Buah the Minister of Trade and the relevant departments, along with all other importers. But when it was announced that the total import licence from my businesses had a value of 500,000 cedis (about £100,000), it was announced as headlines in the Opposition paper, ignoring the fact that this, too, was a drop of 64 percent from the licences Astab had had in previous years. In the following year, 1981, import licences were cut again and my Corporation only received 125,000 cedis worth of licence. But it seemed that the Minister of Trade, had reason to be nervous whenever the figures associated with me were announced!

In some way – perhaps because of the release from an unnatural militay régime – there was a spirit of 'quick money' in the country in those years of 1979-81. The atmosphere, the gossip, was all of the main chance and the shady deal, and this polluted every aspect of life, so that it was assumed that everybody was involved in the activities which – again – everybody heard about. It was when I moved into my new house which was built before the PNP came to power that the wife of a University Professor was driving past it, when she said to her companion 'Don't tell me that a bookseller built that house!' Her companion, a political opponent though, did, I am glad to say, defend me, and said quite correctly that the house had been built by my own construction company, certain parts were panelled by my own carpentry division and decorated by myself and my friends at weekends. It is a beautiful house, and it is the product of the resources I had assembled before my re-entry into politics, by my own hard work in business. But politicians are targets, and the universal phrase was "Must be – otherwise how?" Without any reasons assigned the NDC has taken it over. What a big joke!

Success attracts criticism too, and I was of course at the same time the Chairman of the Ghana Industrial Holdings Corporation, the largest industrial organization in black Africa.

The Central Committee of the People's National Party had recommended to the president that I should be appointed the Chairman of the Ghana Industrial Holdings Corporation. the motion for my appointment was moved by Mr A S A Abban, the Minister of Education, and it was unanimously carried. I did not lobby for the position as I never did in such situations.

I accepted the responsibility because I thought I should accept the challenge of making the state enterprises efficient and profitable, and to run them on sound commercial lines.

My first approach was to ensure that the divisions of GIHOC should no longer be governed by civil service conditions of service. Each division should be set production targets and its annual balance sheet should be published in the Ghanaian papers. The nation would thus be in a position to known which divisions were effective, as well as those which were lagging behind.

It was my duty to ensure that all the members of the Board of Directors of the 22 divisions of GIHOC would not exist by name only; neither were they to be merely ornamental adjuncts to their organizations. In their deliberations and policy formulation, directors were expected to identify themselves with the organization they served. They must know that the successes of the organization or the failures were ultimately their successes or failures as members of boards.

Proceeding from the conduct of board affairs, the top executive and his management team must take the cue. With clearly established criteria, measurable performance, and with quotas and targets clearly set for units of operation periods, management functions could be subjected to quantification. I was determined to ensure that efficiency was rewarded, failures were punished and the unfit were replaced by the more fit.

To equip myself fully for the task, I accepted an invitation to participate in a top management programme in Cambridge University. I realized that management leadership must spring from a position of strength. Knowledge must be replenished and enhanced from time to time. Though my participation was severely criticized by the Opposition parties in Parliament and the press, the result of what I did in Cambridge was rewarding with the visible signs of improvement in the running of GIHOC. The result in the first year was a profit of 25 million cedis, followed by 56 million cedis in the second year.

In all my speeches to the GIHOC workers at all levels, I always insisted that nobody should consider himself above learning and that every use must be made of learning situations. I made arrangements in Cambridge for the facilities to be extended to my management staff.

The biggest challenge which faced me was to take away the GIHOC from the claws of black marketeers and profiteers. I always regarded these elements as dangerous, unpatriotic – even criminal. I realized that they were often highly placed people in all spheres of the nation's life – politicians, journalists, soldiers, lawyers, etc. The most depressing aspect was that some of them were members of my Party, highly placed themselves, or having close connections with highly placed persons in the leadership of the Party. I realized that some people were even using my name for such nefarious purposes. On two occasions, 3 March 1981 and 10 July 1981, I made the Acting Managing Director, Mr C Y Nyonator, draw the attention of all General Managers to the situation where some members of the public were using the names of the Chairman and members of the Corporate Board to seek favours in various subsidiaries.

He emphasized that the letters had become necessary in response to my personal appeal on the issue as a result of persistent reports reaching me that my name was being dragged into those matters.

I am sure no General Manager or Senior Officer will ever say I used my position to take the Corporation's products for my own use – or to use them for influence or favours. And my friends knew I was not ready to help them to get any of the products of GIHOC, without passing through the approved channels.

The essence of the new success of GIHOC was determination, clear objectives and honesty – and minimum interference by the Government. It seemed to me that one of the reasons why this large Corporation had lost so much money in the past was because of continued interference by Government, and that ability to hide behind Government which characterizes all state corporations. When I was Chairman, I kept Ministers out of the Corporation; and I have heard of a Minister refusing to come and see me about the complaints of one of the Deputy Managing Directors, because he knew what reception he would get! The final aim, incidentally, of my strategy, which was never achieved, was to establish some kind of internal bank for the Corporation so that profits could be ploughed into the industrial activities for which it was established, and should not disappear into the maw of Government money. The Rawlings Government has, since 1981, been silent on the affairs of GIHOC. I know that GIHOC was a success; I take this silence as confirmation and as a great compliment.

People quite often dislike a man who appears to be successful in politics. It is very difficult indeed to escape criticism if the impression is created that you live comfortably – I think this was my misfortune. What people forgot was that I had made whatever money I have made through business during the two periods of my life when I have not been in politics. On the two occasions when I went back into politics, in 1959 and 1979, I left my business preoccupation behind me and my income fell. But my businesses have flourished when I have been fully involved with them, and particularly since the days when I began farming and developing my charcoal and sugar cane business; both my businesses and I have prospered together. In particular, it was during the period when I went into school contracting and science equipment, that I opened my book-shops overseas, in the Gambia and in Togo. These flourished and have provided me with sources of foreign exchange, and sources from which I have even been able to import goods into Ghana when Ghana's foreign exchange situation was particu-larly bad. I am not ashamed of being successful in business, and there are things I find myself able to do now, which have been the result of things that I have done in the past; and the result of hard work and good fortune.

When I became a successful businessman, and later when I urged and pursued a policy of economic development through personal effort and commitment, some people have said that I had abandoned my earlier political beliefs. I have not changed my stand on socialism. Time has made it clear to me that the changes and convulsions in Africa, easily termed 'Socialist Revolution', are attempts to repeat what the Western bourgeoisie had achieved in the seventeenth, eighteenth and nineteenth centuries.

The objective of these revolutions was to create the condi-tions in which the accumulation of capital could take place without interference. The fact that they are taking place under the leadership of militant nationalists, often calling themselves 'Marxist-Leninists', or people who my good friend, Peter Enaharo, brilliantly describes as 'dizzy with half-digested les-sons about Socialism', is a reflection of the weakness of the local capitalist class.

National unity, economic growth, and some reduction in social inequality have been fruits of these revolutions. They have not succeeded, however, in breaking the hold of the capitalist world-system on their economies.

The reason why they have failed is not any lack of effort on the part of the régimes concerned. No, the cause of their failure is more fundamental.

I see the modern world economy as an increasingly highly integrated system, of which nation-states are its mere component parts. No economy, however powerful, can escape the pressures of the international system.

When the PNP took power, I thought, in spite of what I have held for socialism for years, that the objective situation required that the only way in which our economy could take off was by drawing on the resources of world capitalism. For example, the most powerful lever for raising the productivity of labour is by installing modern technology. But advanced machinery is produced by advanced countries, and has to be paid for in their own scarce currencies. The easiest way to find the money is to borrow it from the Western banks. This creates a burden on the borrower country, which has to make interest payments, as will as repay the principal.

This means more borrowing, or else finding markets for exports. The effect is to bind the so-called socialist country to the world system. For example, in Cuba, sugar is given priority over industries more important to the country's internal development, because it is an export earner. The result can be seen in the now publicised announcement that Cuba is to renegotiate its $3 billion debt to the West. Creditors are expecting Castro, like Poland's Jaruzelski and Mexico's Madrid, to 'get his house in order' by reducing standards and cutting government spending.

As I see it, the only way in which the grip of the world system can be broken is through a realistic approach to the world economic system, not by pursuing the Utopia of unrealistic revolutions.

The fact is that the enthusiasm that explodes the 're-volutionaries' on to the streets, without direction and organization, blows itself out when the realities of the world situation unfold themselves. Their energy fritters away. Demoralization replaces dynamism.

DESTABILIZATION PROCESSES

In the face of our efforts, the slow progress we were making in solving the country's economic problems went hand in hand with political instability, and though some of this was reflected in Parliament, most of the problems came, unfortunately, from outside the formal political system – and a lot of it from one man – J J Rawlings.

There were so many *coups d'etat* attempts between 1979 and 1981 that I have a problem as to whether to enumerate all of them or mention only the more significant ones. I think we should limit the list to the really serious ones. I think we must expect the fact that hardly a month passed by, during the period, without an effort by some soldiers, inspired of course by Jerry Rawlings, to seize power and establish what they perceived as a government of 'ordinary workers and soldiers'.

To understand the years between 1979 and 1981, we have to accept the fact that Rawlings never wanted to hand over power in September 1979 and literally had to be forced to do so. After the hand-over, his intentions were clear: to come back a second time. In fact his target date was April 1980.

Before I go into the details of the coup plots, I want to stress the point that J J Rawlings subverted the soldiers by impressing them with the power they could secure and by promising them the loot when the coup was successful. He also exploited the natural gulf between officers and other ranks to achieve his aims. His other strategy was to exploit every political situation in the country, use the media skillfully and beam the message in simple fashion to the soldier in the barracks, who was expected to take up the fight by rising up as he had done on 4 June 1979.

The Limann administration was bedevilled with so many attempts at coups from 1979 to 1981 that it is a wonder it was not toppled earlier.

In October 1979, under the guise of appealing for funds for the welfare of troops killed or wounded in the 4 June 1979 uprising, Rawlings was to call the troops to mutiny all over Accra, seize power and incite his return to power. In this campaign, the Air Force station, Accra and 5th Battalion were to provide the bulk of the troops; units were to rally their supporters in the various units, to back the initial action. The coup failed through the arrest and discharge from the service of the conspirators.

In November 1979, anticipating the general confusion

caused by the jail-break which he inspired, Rawlings and his bodyguards were to go into camp and urge his followers to seize power. This plan was foiled because when the jail-break took place, Rawlings was brought in to meet members of the Government and PNP leaders, and he pledged his loyalty to the government. Later on, he said I had 'twisted his arm' to take this pledge.

The months of November and December 1979 were a period of phony coup attempts. Every Friday preceding every weekend, reports were fed into the Armed Forces from the Rawlings camp that the 'boys' were going to do it again. This created a scare and caused panic among soldiers and their families. But this should be seen as part of a carefully designed plan to wear down forces loyal to the Government, create frustration among them and so encourage troops who were fed up with the many guard duties they were performing and, as a result, to mutiny.

It was suggested he should strike between 14 December and 31 December, using Rawlings loyalists in Air Force Station, but he postponed this idea after persuasion from some of his supporters, who told him the time was not ripe for such a venture.

March 1980 started with a major conspiracy involving elements from all the major units in Accra. It was led by a Sgt Henry Sowah. The key planners were eleven other ranks and one officer of the rank of a Lieutenant, and it was timed for execution on 29 March 1980. It was foiled. The planners were jailed and their associates, numbering over thirty, were all dismissed from the Armed Forces.

What was termed 'The Tantoungi Plot' was planned in May 1980. This was led by an LAC nicknamed 'Tantoungi', and was to buy out the police personnel at the Broadcasting House to enable the leader to gain access to the Broadcasting Station and make a broadcast on 15 May to the nation and to call on troops to rise up against the Government. Rawlings was to be invited to broadcast to the nation, on the successful implementation of the plan and was to become Head of State. There was to be considerable troop movement on that day and certain key military and political figures were to be executed. The whole plan was foiled by Military Intelligence. A plot similar to the above was foiled in June 1980. It was effected by elements from 1st Battalion in Tema.

There were a series of coup attempts which were nipped in the bud from July to September 1981. They involved troops in the 5th Battalion, the Air Force Stations at Accra and Takoradi, and the Field Engineers. The most notable one among them was the Adu Effah conspiracy which was also designed to put Rawlings back in power in July 1980. Corporal Adu Effah was in the Sowah group, but had been asked to lie low and reactivate his plan in case the Sowah one failed.

An assassination strategy was adopted from October 1980 to February 1981. When Rawlings and his group realized that attempts at taking over power by the route described above had signally failed, they changed their strategy. The plan called for the selected assassination of key military personnel and civilians and so terrorize the population to such an extent that Ghanaians would call on Rawlings as the only one capable of maintaining law and order. This approach was also foiled.

In May 1981, Rawlings modified his assassination plot and came up with a new idea. It was set for execution on 22 May 1981. The Chief of Defence Staff was to be kidnapped in his house. He was then to be forced to call all his Service Commanders and the Director of Military Intelligence to a meeting in his house. On their arrival all were to be captured and held for ransom. the Chief of Defence staff was then to be compelled to ask the President, the Vice President and the Cabinet to step down and to invite Rawlings to take over. The captured senior officers were then to be executed as a warning to all those who might be tempted to resist the take-over.

This was followed by 'The Buller Plan' which was a long-term strategy designed for implementation in 1982/83. If it had been allowed to develop, Ghana would have had a guerilla warfare situation on her hands. Guerillas would have been trained on a farm at Okpoglo. It also involved the clandestine training and equipping of a carefully selected group of pro-Rawlings cadres in camps near Teshie and Nsawam; and their use as terrorists, to wage a campaign of terror against selected targets. Arms and money for these projects were expected to have come from the Libyans. Later, it was discovered from security agencies that 20,000,000 CFA was paid into the account of a Ghanaian businessman of Togo extraction, based in London, in Lomé Togo, for the benefit of the organizers of this plan. Weapons for this project were already in a secret cache on the

Legon/Kwabenya road. Security agencies knew the location and were closely waiting for the group to draw near it.

Buller, who was in close touch with Rawlings and Tsikata, was arrested and deported from Ghana. Rawlings was arrested for questioning in connection with allegations made against him by Buller. When he was detained, his followers contacted elements in the Air Force Station, Accra, to strike, on the pretext that the Government wanted to kill Rawlings and disband the Air Force. LACs Ghafa, Dzibolusu and Deku were preparing to stage a coup when they were arrested.

In June 1981, elements from Takoradi and Accra attempted to 'strike'. LAC Martey Mensah of Takoradi Air Force Station, who was on leave at the time, was one of the main linkmen with Rawlings. This plan was to involve the use of Rawlings' former bodyguards as the main force in the coup. But one of them leaked details of the plan. It was set for 1st July 1981.

In July 1981 the Rawlings group came up with the final plan: Rawlings was to sneak into the barracks at midnight, go to the Recce Regiment and sleep in the room of one of his Recce supporters. Then, in the early hours of the morning, use elements form his group in Recce to hijack the duty armoured cars, seize key parts of the camp and on a pre-arranged signal, get his supporters in Takoradi and Tema to come to his aid. The plan which was set for August/September was however postponed. It was to be postponed several times between September and December 1981. In the course of investigations by the Military Intelligence, some of the conspirators in Takoradi, Accra and Ho were arrested in December 1981. In fact, this forced Rawlings to postpone the coup to 15 January 1982, but the time changed again to 31 December 1981 as a result of pressure from the Nungua branch of the 4 June Movement and from certain politicians of the People's National Party.

I must emphasize that I was in a dilemma when I decided to look through the mass of details of coup attempts between September 1979 and December 1981. I was forced to be purposefully selective. The criterion I used was to select the attempts I thought had a potential of overthrowing the constitutional order between 1979 and 1981. There were so many others that are not worth mentioning because they were dealt with at lower levels. Taken altogether, however, they tended to create a psychosis of fear and tension and – I have no doubt in my mind – contributed to the general state of insecurity in Ghana during that period.

There were other political convulsions which created the state of insecurity. In August 1980, certain tendentious outpourings in a Ghanaian journal gave a signal to the smouldering undercurrent of disruptive forces which were seeking adherents to mobilize, in order to serve the ends of dividing the PNP. Under the cloak of 'Nkrumah loyalists', the voices of these socially discredited pedlars of presumed doctrines were being raised on the air and in the press, purporting to be in the representative voice of the people; purporting, indeed, to represent the message of PNP canvassers at the 1979 General Election.

The claim that the PNP was an off shoot of Kwame Nkrumah's was taking on new constructions; namely, that PNP was synonymous with CPP. We were expected to believe that the effigy of Kwame Nkrumah and the ideology of the CPP had been those which were hoisted to win the elections.

By extension, the President, Dr Hilla Limann, must be seen, and must conduct the affairs of his office, much as if he were a carbon copy of the historical Nkrumah. If the mischievous propagators of these gospels took the trouble to think at all, they appeared to ignore or forget the fact that Nkrumah himself, had he been alive at the time, and had he remained in effective control of Ghan's affairs, might have had his views and ideology on social control considerably modified and transformed in keeping with the changing and changed realities of the day.

Not only were a number of proponents of Nkrumahism, and for that matter, Marxism, uninformed about the contents of the ideologies they effected to espouse, but also they had not kept abreast with the breath-taking lessons which were occurring in the ranks of Marxists, Maoists, Leninists, Trotskyites and even in Tanzania and Guinea. The developments in France, Spain and Italy, going under the term 'Euro-Communism', might hardly have had dawned on our Ghanaian ideologues.

I worked closely by the side of Kwame Nkrumah in giving expression to his emergent and evolving ideas on Nkrumahism, particularly in my capacity as Editor of *The Spark*, the ideological exponent of the prevailing and emerging views on a homegrown doctrine believed to meet the peculiar circumstances of an ex-colonial country like Ghana. Nkrumah, for one thing, allowed for the Euro-Judaic-Christian, Islamic and other ideological, philosphical and cultural buffeting which the country had experienced within the period of the colonial contact and subjugation. The groping for a more fitting, localized terminology than Marxism-Leninism accounted for the adoption, as a matter of convenience, of Nkrumahism. Those who were familiar with the ideological evolution of the Leader through his formative years at College to the age of maturity as a national Leader and an international personality, could not fail to notice the phases of growth and subtle transformation of outlook and knowledge, as his ideas gradually crystallized. One could not say that, even in his final days in Conakry, the process of crystallization of thought and ideas had reached finality. Nkrumah would be the last to say that his ideas were sacrosanct and that they were infallible for all time!

Assuming, for purposes of argument, that the historical Nkrumah had bequeathed to posterity in Ghana a permanent blue-print for an ideology, and assuming that the PNP and its living Leader were a carbon copy of the foregone entities, how do we reconcile these things with Ghana's national Constitution which forbade the use and application of political replicas drawn from the past?

The simplistic interpretation and post-mortem of the 1979 Election results which claimed that success was accountable to the CPP and Nkrumah myth, seemed to forget that decisions of voters spring from a most complex of factors and motivations. I make bold to include in the list of the factors which won for us the victory at the polls, the spectre of brand new faces and names and personalities, which the PNP fielded. It was nothing short of a scoop which PNP made to the utter suprise and discomfiture of rival parties. PNP utilized the seasoned resources of old leaders to offer fresh leaders in response to the mood of the times. That sleight of hand outwitted our competitors and won converts to the Party.

Both local sceptics and overseas doubters found the PNP fielding new, unadulterated, politically unblemished human material. If it was honest to goodness respectability they looked out for, they got it in the PNP cadre of Party and Government officials. The outcome was confidence in the Party and Government on the part of outsiders.

For over a year we had let outblown claims float abut concerning the kind of support which brought Dr Hilla Limann into power. The hardly-veiled blackmail which certain power-hungry, influence-hungry, past masters at knocking of the heads of those who stood in their way, had it that, unless Dr Limann behaved as a carbon copy of Kwame Nkrumah his civilian predecessor, they the power-brokers would pull the carpet from under Limann's feet.

In an article crying for my head, T D Baffoe former Editor-in-Chief of the *Ghanaian Times* suddenely permitted certain figures he had all along condemned as most evil to take on respectability and honour, which, he threatened Limann listen to, or else . . . his words were:

'If he will not listen the CPP will be well-advised to withdraw its support and take to the country and reorganize the true CPP and leave Okutwer, Batsa, de Graft Johnson and their bed-fellows to govern with their skeleton PNP as they dream of Arab Petro-dollar cash for development as if it is easily picked from minarets.'

To me, our major task should have been to call off the bluff, clear the air, assert leadership and mobilize support which stood ready to rally behind the Party. Other well-wishers, who were not sure whether the noise makers of the Party would succeed in using the PNP, and with it, the whole nation, to thy-kingdom-come of ideological adventurism, watched on the side-lines.

It was time to clear the political air with a refreshing approach which need not depart from the policies enunciated in the Party Manifesto and in the address of Dr Limann to the Kumasi Party Congress.

I always held the view that if we prepared the ground carefully, a complete realignment of political forces could have emerged and the platform fo the Party would have seen the marshalling of people of rare expertise who were held back for being unsure of our direction and permanent stand.

I had occasion to tell Dr Limann that every Leader has his achievements and mistakes to account for. He must not oblige those who would like to mislead him into mixing the mistakes of a predecessor with his own. The more enlightened promoters and organizers of the Party had stressed the more worthy, the more positive and the good in what Nkrumah did and stood for. These enlightened, selective builders of our Party would not ask Limann to adopt lock, stock and barrel, the policies and ideologies of a past reality which would not fit today's realities.

Since PNP was not an ideological party, and showed itself as essentially a nationalist group consisting of conflicting interests; leftist, centralists, and conservative elements, one expected Limann to hold the line between the factions at both ends of his Party membership, and to thread the path of consensus and politics which united rather than divided the people he led. One thought that if nature and circumstances would have carried over those initial promises and prospects into the future which the man, Dr Limann had brought over to his office of high calling, then, there was a chance that the hopes and aspirations for a better Ghana would not have been dashed in disappointment. Then, indeed, the future might reasonably be expected to bud and sprout blossoms of prosperity, peace and happiness the like of which had eluded the people of Ghana these many past years of anguish and adversity. It was obvious that some of the "old knights of the shires" found me irritating and pushy. It was unfortunate that they never thought of new ways to approach old problems.

Since the coup of 31 December 1981, I have been assailed by friends and foes with the question of Limann's leadership. As former editor of *The Spark* and one of the journalists closely identified with Kwame Nkrumah's rule, I am always asked to compare the leadership of Kwame Nkrumah with Hilla Limann.

I hold the view that it is unrealistic for certain critics to suggest that Limann should adopt a pace and style of leadership that conforms with some set moulds. It is mere fancy believing that Dr Limann or, for that matter, any leader, can be other than himself. Though Ghanaians like other Africans like visible Presidency, I thought it was not justified to expect Limann to take the posture of Kwame Nkrumah.

It should have been obvious to most people that nothing but futility would result, if the mild-mannered man were to try to bear the garb of Kwame Nkrumah. The truth is the image and charisma a person carries, issues from the total personality of the leader himself.

I am always convinced that Dr Limann knows himself, too well, the danger in the process of living it up like the man he is not. He strikes me as knowing how fast it was possible to hasten under the complex and difficult circumstances confronting his administration. Strewn with the debris of the virtual scorched-earth consumption of the preceding military regimes, the ground needs winnowing and re-sowing before one could expect new shoots.

Those who were closely associated with Dr Limann could not but notice his sensitivity to the suffering and long patience of Ghanaians. He was in tune with the yearnings and aspirations of the helpless urban and rural people. He knew that it was cold comfort to expect a suffering person to be told to wait. Urgent as the need for remedies no doubt was, Dr Limann was all too well aware that wrong or misapplied solutions, done under the steam of haste, could worsen the suffering and waste the limited resources.

Whenever I am forced to answer the question whether I thought Dr Limann represented presidential leadership in an era of crisis, I start with the story of Confucius, who came upon a woman weeping bitterly by a grave by the side of Mount Thai. He went close to her and, bending down asked: "What may your sorrow be for which you wail so bitterly?" The woman replied: "Oh, Sir, my sorrow is sorrow on sorrow." "Sorrow on sorrow, you said?" "Yes," replied the forlorn woman "Here, at this very spot a tiger has killed my husband's father, then my husband, and latterly my son died in the same way." Confucius said: "Why don't you leave this place, then?" She answered, saying: "There is no oppressive government here!" "Ah, indeed," observed Confucius, "you spoke truly; oppressive government is more terrible than the most terrrible tiger." To me, political leadership has to do with the exercise of power. State power of an elected, presidential kind may take the form of arbitrary exercise of power, or limited exercise of power. Where presidential prerogative is unlimited, and the population is submissive, they may follow their national leader into dictatorship. And where the various arms of state, namely, the Armed Forces, the Police, the Courts and the mass communications media, are safely under the unfettered control of the leader, the leader's exercise of state power may become more and more oppressive, especially if any subject were to be so misguided as to dare oppose the absolute leader!

As a matter of fact, an elected president may be electorally predestined to autocracy and oppressive rule. This is when the single candidate role presents voters with no option of a choice. The rubber stamp electoral procedure frees the candidate from competition. Young African states are doing this in the name of national unity, ethnic integration and national stability. Justification is found in the fact that the virtual emergency condition in which nation-building involves a young state admits of no luxury of opposing political parties.

Or else a perfectly legitimate constitutional system may make provision for a president who can claim wide dicretionary power in times of either war or threatened war.

As Bertrand Russell, in his work *Power – A New Social Analysis* pointed out: 'War is the chief promoter of despotism, since it obstructs the establishment of a system of responsible power'. Continuing, the philosopher tells us: '. . . all war, especially modern war, promotes dictatorship by causing the timid to seek a leader and by converting the bolder spirits from a society into a pack.' Bertrand Russell was thinking of a pack of pliant sheep! He spoke of how the risk of war causes a certain kind of mass hysteria, mass collective hysteria, which all too often plays into the hands of despotism.

Even under time-tested democracies in the older, industrialized and commercialized nations of Europe, fear of imminent catastrophe was to create panic, leading to the coalescing of parliamentary political parties into a joint-party or national government.

Cut out to be a war-time leader, Sir Winston Churchill held sway over his countrymen with a gift of oratory which could be contained only by the Allied High Command. The equivalent of opium which he administered to his people was rhetoric and propaganda. Common fear and danger, common hatred of the enemy and collective hysteria were such as turned otherwise strong and questioning minds into credulous believers of what war-time propaganda dished out to them. Churchill's side did win the war.

Another example of a crisis leader was Adolf Hitler, who seduced a whole nation into bigotry. He played on the emotions of his countrymen, smarting under the humiliations of defeat in post-First World War Germany, to create an atmosphere of fear, rage and collective excitement in which people blindly followed him, whilst he took advantage of their trust to establish himself as a tyrant. Racial hatred of the Jews resulted in inhuman slaughter in gas chambers of millions of Jews. Bombarded consistently by psychological missiles, a nation's outlook was screwed to revenge, territorial grabbing in the name of *Lebensraum* (living space) and Aryan purity of a mythical Teutonic stock. With a creed like a flag held aloft, and dogmatic indoctrination, fanatics of "new dispensation", so-called, marched on at the bidding of the leader, the Fuehrer of Hitler's *National Socialism*. National Socialism as a party swept out of existence, or drove underground, all dissenting viewpoints and parties to prepare the ground for the holocaust which the Second World War unleashed upon mankind.

What was that rare quality which certain individuals in their society possessed that would distinguish them from the vast majority who were content to do the bidding of a Cromwell, A Mussolini, a Napoleon, an Alexander the Great of Macedonia? Each of these crisis leaders believed, with each leadership success, that he was an ordained, anointed, minister come to save, to redeem, to liberate his people form real or imagined enemies. Each had a firm faith in his star. Each possessed abundant self-confidence, abundant skill in combining the fear and greed of his fellow men and women with situational opportunites. Each was quick to take advantage of offerings of power. These leaders also had a quality, call it charisma if you please, by which they galvanized the fear and greed of those around them into pursuing goals which met the personal needs of the revolutionary leaders. It so happens that the lust for power and authority over others, which the foregoing leaders aspired after, happened to coincide with the craving that their followers as knowing the answers.

As fear thickens with approaching danger imagined doom, most people all too willingly sign away their liberty, self-reliance and independent action to a leader and, as followers, they feel relieved that the leader will repel the onslaught of the coming threat or danger. Did Ghanaians not rush to the streets to hail 'revolutionary' leaders as leaders who, by a wave of their swagstaff, would save Ghana?

What are the inner drives which motivate the leader of a people, whether in times of crisis or in normal times? If you look closely, the goal towards which the inner drives of a leader impel him is, as like as not, that of acquiring *power*. Power here means the apparatus, the means, by which effective leadership-influence is exercised over followers. Craving for power is so strong and insistent that the more they have of it, the better they feel. Power affords them a sense of fulfilment.

For those upon whom leadership is thrust, as by election or by popular appointment, the *glory* of the position makes up for power. A traditional leader who has not fought for the position, or a King who ascends to the royal throne, has customary *influence* and is satisfied with his influence over his people. There is nothing naked or raw about the exercise of influence over people. Influence descends and speaks almost as if one were applying the influence to oneself. In the former monarchical age, the power and the glory were combined in the person of the monarch. Some Kings did rise to the occasion when disaster struck, when an earthquake, a hurricane, a flood over a vast terrain, or an epidemic, struck or when an enemy attacked.

A far cry, did you say, from the case of a mild-mannered presidential leader like the constitutional Chief Executive and Head of State of Ghana's Third Republic! Hemmed in by checks and balances, the power and the authority he wielded were regulated and limited. The constitutional President as by law exalted, was expected to play the role of a leader in a normal time, not a crisis leader. The Constitution under which Dr Hilla Limann ruled was first and foremost designed for now and posterity; not for a limited crisis period. The President could neither levy taxes nor continue in office beyond a specified period, nor perform the duties of a judge, nor impose laws. He had his presidential track laid out along which he must operate.

All of this was perfectly understandable. The Constitution of the Third Republic, like that of the United States of America and Nigeria next door, was at the instance of a revolution. It was in response to, or in reaction against, an intolerable past when abuse of power was exercised; a past upon which Ghana was presumed to have turned its back for good. A past in which those who came to liberate, to redeem, to cleanse out society free of filth and corruption and greed, proceeded to excel in the very things which had afflicted the people of Ghana. Leaders in a presidential, executive chair, in our recent past, paraded the national stage, each in an era of crisis. Blood did certainly flow; but had the society been cleansed of the malady which had afflicted it?

The test of our time was whether we were prepared to work the Constitution through, and whether support for the President under a democratic system of government would be forthcoming. Did the separate arms of state pick up the pace of urgency which the President led up with? The Constitution of the Third Republic was predicated to operate on the basis of consensus. How else could it work with its numerous autonomous organs which were accountable to the Constitution and to no-one else?

If this was the model of 'Presidential Leadership' in an era of crisis, how do I answer the question? Intensely sincere and deeply commited as Dr Limann unquestionably was to his constitutional charge and pledge, he saw his role as that of containing the 'excited times', to bring sanity and reason into the economic shambles which he inherited and to guide Ghana on with wisdom and tolerance out of, as it were, the tempestuous sea; and to bring his people to the dry land of lush green pastures which was their due!

ON THE WAY OUT

On 30 December 1981, I held meetings with the divisional General Managers of the Ghana Industrial Holdings Corporation in Accra to review their work for the year and examine their financial projections in detail. The meetings were useful.

I then drove to the house of my old friend, Alex Aidoo, a lawyer and the Chairman of the Daily Graphic Corporation, and told him that I was going to spend the New Year at my home in Manya Krobo. Just before I drove up there, I remember, I met two friends, Mr Justice Charles Coussey and Eric Otu, now Ghana's Ambassador in the United States.

Charles Coussey said 'What do you think of all these rumours about coups? There are too many.' My reply was that I had heard the rumours and had a feeling that the country was not safe. A remark I was to remember.

Most coups in Ghana are coups by radio, and I always turn on the radio at 6 o'clock in the morning to see what the news is and to see whether we would be safe for the day. On New Year's Eve, I turned on the radio at 8 am and there was no particualarly interesting news. I decided to remain in bed for a while, reading, and because I was planning a New Year Box for the local Party workers, I sent my driver back to Accra to bring some materials I had left behind. Soon after the driver had left, the houseboy from my house in Accra rushed in saying that something was happening in the capital and that somebody had called twice, at 5am and again at 7.30 am at the house, to ask where I was. He said that there was firing in the camp and some confusion, and the story was that the Chairman of the Party and the Vice President had both left their homes, although there was nothing on the radio. He had immediately decided to tell me this news and had come to me as fast as he could in a local bus.

Although nothing seemed very definite, I thought it best to get myself out of the house, and I took myself up to the school house, nearby, to wait. At 11am the news was confirmed; Flight Lt Rawlings was on the radio announcing the overthrow of the Government. What we had half expected and had discussed in Accra had come about.

I decided to go up into the hills behind the town – the first time I had ever been there. Taking only a small bag with some papers and my travel documents, I walked for about five miles into the hills to an isolated farm. And although I only met one person on the journey, an old man carrying wood, the first messenger who came up from the town to keep me in touch said that within two hours of leaving, everyone in the town knew where I was. The same system of messengers brought me the news that the troops came at 6 pm – three truck loads with a Captain in charge, a Captain who, when told that I was not at home, had said "Thank God". The next day I decided I must move and travelled, with a lot of help from a lot of people – both civilian and military – to a spot near the border where I decided to wait a little longer and see whether the coup was really successful and whether there was any chance of safe return. I received a message saying that the loyal troops were under pressure from new Russian weapons and were likely to have to surrender. A friend said "You have done a lot for your country, but you have been misundersstood. Don't take any risks, because they won't give you a chance to explain". And that was a military friend! So, with the help of many kind people I became an exile; safe, but an exile. The only remaining accident on the journey which was exaggerated in Ghana was when valuable manuscripts that I was carrying fell into the water. I retrieved some of them, – damp, but in good condition.

In the first six months, I thought I should not have gone into exile. I am a Ghanaian and should stay at home to the storms of Ghana, not grimly but willingly. I should let myself be stamped in Ghana's experience. I should not be automatically lumped in peoples' minds with the infamous politicians in Ghana. But the warning to stay out came to me from a current joke in Teheran. It is about the fox who was hurrying out of town. Someone asked the reason for such haste. The fox said: 'In that town they kill foxes that have three balls.' 'But have you got three balls?' he asked. 'No,' replied the fox, 'But they kill you first and count your balls afterwards.'

The military investigation techniques which rely on torture, methods which range from beating on the feet and burning with cigarette stubs to the use of electricity with the aim of extracting a confession, which subsequently followed the military take-over justified my accepting to be in exile.

Day by day the Ghanaian scene shows the growth of three types of political leadership: those who show they are out of their minds; those who appear to be going out of their minds; and those who indicate that they have no minds to go out of. This still re-enforces my stand that I should reluctantly stay in exile.

Looking back for a moment, I must say a word about some of the people I have met in Ghanaian politics. In considering the character sketches of some of the politicians I met along the road of political life in Ghana, I angled them to demonstrate certain points. There were very useful people in my life who I do not intend to mention, not because I am not grateful for their helping hand or have no regard to their views, but because I do not think they should be mentioned now. I have deliberately ignored those who I think it is in their interest for me to refrain from mentioning. They are the shabby bunch!

In the days of Nkrumah, I had to string along with my journalist colleagues and the emerging ideologues of the Party. I dare say that Kofi Badu, T D Baffoe, Kwesi Amoako-Atta, Eric Heyman, Kweku Akwei, Ekow Ampah, K Budu Acquah and Kojo Addison were my colleagues. In fact we were described by the press as 'the socialist boys'. As a group, we believed in the justness of our cause and we were dedicated and loyal to Kwame Nkrumah. They deserve more than a fleeting reference. Some of them were very good and some of them behaved like snakes on eggs. In dealing with them I always put my head up and have my guts where it should be. But T D Baffoe took me on as his political enemy. A close study disclosed that he thought I should be like him. It was unfortunate that he constantly kept as his abiding enemy, success, and kept fighting those who tended to take strides ahead of him. His handicap was that though he had built enthusiasm for the cause of Nkrumah he did not build an intellectual base to sustain him. He gradually reduced himself to the level of a wily, theatrical, tragi-comic, political figure. I constantly ignored his open attacks on me because I thought I should not be detracted by trivialities.

The Ghana political scene has produced some very useful politicians who have convinced me that Ghana could rely on them. You may disagree with them, but there was always the feeling that they are patriotic and very willing to work for Ghana. In the parties to which I did not belong, I found J H Mensah, da Rocha, Kweku Folson, Dr John Bilson, William Ofori Atta, G Amarteifio, A R T Madjitey, Professor Adu Boahen, belonging to this category. I held Mr K A Gbedemah in high esteem but his political views were not acceptable to me. In the early stages of his political life, he was a straight shooter and a shrewd judge of useful political moments. But in the last few years he appeared to have ignored the way to test public reaction to things and he gradually threw out his astute way of putting his spin on things.

In the Party I belonged to, I found a host of dedicated colleagues. Outside the political parties, I found Anthony Kobena Woode, Professor Eddie Ayensu, Robet Hayfron Benjamin, Frimpong Ansah, Professor Lamousie-Smith Dr Francis Nkrumah, Thomas Mensah and G Adali Mortty. Politically honest Ghana definitely needs them.

There are some non-political friends who did a lot to help me see myself as I should in politics. Kwame Sarbah, K Nyame Kumi and Dr Felix Konotoy Ahulu. I owe them a lot of gratitude on my way up in politics.

When I told a friend that I was going to write a book, he asked me whether I intended running down J J Rawlings. I told him that though I do in fact assess him as a spiteful and vindictive busybody, I would like the dust around him to settle down. there are some fine colleagues of his in the AFRC who have done enough to spare Ghana a bloodbath. They have made the assessment of Rawlings quite difficult. A typical example is Major Boakye Djan, who has fine political views.

In the heat of the colonial struggle, so many people were thrown on to the political arena. The anti-colonial struggle politician may not necessarily succeed in nation building. There were those elements of the Kwame Nkrumah era who, because they could not make it, hanged the blame on those who tried to make it.

The trade union movement was a breeding ground for these elements. They were essentially demagogues who carved out a reputation for themselves by voicing their grievances with slanderous attacks on all and sundry. these were the elements who made us ran into rough weather.

J K Tettegah used to be the Secretary-General of the TUC. He took the TUC to the pro-Western ICFTU and later withdrew and built alliance with the WFTU. He was removed to the Builders' Brigade by Kwame Nkrumah, pushed over to the All African Trade Union federation and finally found himself on the good side of the 1966 coup makers who toppled Kwame Nkrumah. When he was disenchanted with the 1966 coup makers, he rushed to Tanzania, where President Julius Nyerere gave him a job. He was later thrown out from Dar es Salaam so he went to Conakry to make peace with Kwame Nkrumah. After going through the agony of recanting everything he said against Kwame Nkrumah, he decided to settle in Cairo. He took advantage of General Acheampong's coup which over-threw Dr K A Busia's government and returned to Ghana. He made an attempt to topple the regime of General Acheampong and was sentenced to death after a trial for treason. I footed the bill for the legal services he had during his trial. He was pardoned after the fall of Acheampong and decided to join the PNP and found himself for a short spell in the Central Committee. Posing as the champion of the people, he made no concrete proposals which would help the people, but dwelt on slanders and exaggerated instances of corruption; not to stamp these out, but to furnish help to the military to topple the democratically elected Government of Limann. Today he is on the right side of Rawlings. He has been appointed Ghana's Ambassador to Moscow. He plays the cynical game of political opportunism. His actions are always politically corrosive.

In Parliament in Ghana I respected the views of Dr James Ofori Atta, Atta Kescon, Joe Hyde and Peter Adjetey. There were a few young fighting ones who time would have done a lot to build.

As regards the Members of Parliament in general in the Limann era, they did not make the effort to outgrow the stage where Parliament is merely a glorified debating society, providing a platform for the exhibitionism of politicians, acting as the battleground for narrow sectional aims, incapable of defending the needs and hopes of the people. It appeared some of them were growing paranoid and therefore took delight in bisarre fracas.

I hold the strong view that an MP must take part in the practical life of his constituents; the MP must be able to listen. An MP is not doing his constituents a favour by listening to them, he is only doing his political duty. By listening to the people, by seeking their advice, by asking for their judgement about problems, we make democracy alive for them.

Every constituent must be helped to feel that he can approach his MP on all kinds of problems and be assured of a friendly hearing. Arrogance, lording it over people, has no part in a nation's life.

The trust of the people is the most precious possession of any representative, to be won by devotion to his duty to them and his practical example.

Among the Cabinet Ministers I held in high esteem were Harry Sawyer, Dr Amon Nikoi, Joe Reindorf, Dr Isaac Chinebuah and Professor Benneh. Time would have built the best out of them. the enthusiasm of Dr John Nabila, Francis Buah, Torto, Dr K Ocran, Wolf Tagoe, Dr Francis Acquah and A L Djabetey was remarkable. Francis Badjie, the High Commissioner in London, distinguished himself as a enthusiastic worker. Dr Ivan Addae-Monsah, the General Secretary of the PNP was very efficient. He was honest and meticulous in his financial administration. He fought what he did not accept with brilliant distaste. He fought for the youth and he always stood against all adult attempts to straight jacket youth. I always wish he, Dr. Arthur, the secretary of Dr Limann and Sam Cudjoe, the western Regional Minister would get the opportunity to re-enter Ghana politics. They have a lot to do for Ghana.

I had known Joe de Graft Johnson for some time, having met him through a mutual friend, Joseph Sackey, then Principal Secretary of the Ministry of Foreign Affairs. The three of us used to meet quite regularly, and became close personal friends, getting a good idea of each other's thoughts and feelings on many subjects. I grew to appreciate de Graft Johnson's ideas and to appreciate the quickness of his mind. He was an engineer both by education and profession, but he read widely outside his subject and became as well informed as he was intelligent. As he was a genial and cheerful man, people often thought he was not serious, but when one became close to him one realized his true qualities.

Joe de Graft Johnson had originally joined the SDF, thinking that it was going to develop as the true people's party, but he soon realized his mistake, and I was responsible for the discussions that brought him into the PNP where, as member for Cape Coast, he made friends very easily and, by the time of the Kumasi conference, was well known throughout the Party.

After I had resisted the lobby to draft me as Vice President, I started lobbying for Joe de Graft Johnson for that post. The father of the party, Egala, who was, like Joe de Graft Johnson, a tall man, liked him and the result was that de Graft Johnson became our candidate for the Vice Presidency and eventually the Vice President by a big majority. He is an honest man and one who, throughout his career, had been determined to live up to the high standards of his distinguished family – a family which has been a great support to him, and has kept him from many of those dubious activities which entrap many people in politics. Joe de Graft Johnson was new to politics but worked hard and assiduously, travelling and speaking a great deal in support of Limann administration and when I heard him in 1981 he had developed a fine platform style and had built on his natural affability a fine appreciation of the popular mood and of the reactions of a crowded audience. At the same time he moved to the centre of the Party's affairs, and was for example joint Chairman of the UNC/PNP meetings which, after the alliance was held in my house. It was shocking to hear that after the Rawlings coup of December 1981, Joe de Graft Johnson had been badly beaten and was held in harsh conditions in an ordinary goal.

As one moves along the international political scene one is bound to meet different shades of people. They either helped to get you going or assiduously worked to run you down and therefore made your work difficult. I am just showing how they influenced my work. I have already mentioned some people as far as they were directly involved in some actions of mine in Ghana. Outside Ghana, I met Col M Gadaffi at a stage when he was just getting his feet into politics. He was young and was in his political formative years. It would be unfair to him if I referred to the extent to which he made any impact on me or the political scene.

In my early political life, which was mainly on the Left, I met Cheddi and Ruth Jagan of Guyana. We were close friends and I admired their dogged fight against British colonialism. they are firm with what they find as solutions to their problems.

Our generation found a new youth of Africa; we were close to each other in ideas and were determined to end colonialism in Africa, I must mention some of them again; Mamoudou Gologo of Mali, Humphrey Mulembea, Simon Kapwepwe, Munu Sipalo and the Wina brothers of Zambia, Oscar Kambona, Salah Salim and Mohamed Badu of Tanzania, Oginga Odinga and Tom Mboya of Kenya, S G Ikoku, Ayo Adebayo, Tony Enaharo, Alao Aka Bashurun, Mmodu, Gogo Nzeribe, Goodluck Otegbeye, Olu Smith, Ade Thomas and a host of brilliant youth in Nigeria Garba Jahumpa of Gambia Dr Mondale of Mozambique, and Amilcar Cabral of Guinea. When I became the Secretary-General of the all African Union of Journalists, I worked very closely with Jean Dean of Guinea, as the President. He was hard working and brilliant. The word goes that he died under strange circumstances in Conakry.

Outside the Africa scene, I always keep the memory of my useful meetings with President Sukarno of Indonesia and his Foreign Minister, Mr Subandrio. Though time has swept them aside, I personally learnt a lot from them. They built useful contacts with Nkrumah and I played my humble part as the main link between them. I made so many trips to Djakarta.

In the early stages of the efforts to build a platform for African Unity, we were regularly carrying messages to President Nasser of Egypt, Haile Selassie of Ethiopia, Modiboo Keita of Mali, and Maga of Dahomey, who were very close to Kwame Nkrumah.

In the period of Limann's administration, I made useful trips to Mexico to meet President Lopez Portillo, to Nigeria to meet President Shagari and to the Gambia to meet President D Jawara. The missions were to foster good relations with those countries. In the case of Mexico, an agreement for a five year oil credit was due to be signed in January 1982.

THE FUTURE

So ends my political story, if such it can be called. I have written this book not to instruct or entertain, still less to make money. No. I wrote simply to explore my own experience. Sometimes it was a matter of just settling the bare facts of my own past. Much more happened that I cannot tell. It would be difficult to define anything that I have personally achieved through all these. I must confess that there was so much to do, but so little done; even the firm foundations which were laid for future wonderful edifices of national progress, were all destroyed through callousness and jealousy. It is hard not to have an uneasy conscience about what my country has gone through. Like every politician in Ghana, I bore a share of the blame for the present state of Ghana. Throughout the years, we had tried, and we had done much. I dare say that our failure is not as shameful as that of those who could have helped, but would not try. Still, blaming others is no more than an extenuation. Every Ghanaian must look to his own conscience.

Our national failure is in many fields: economic, intellectual, moral. How can we find a path of change?

When Dr Hilla Limann was inaugurated as President of Ghana he drove to Black Star Square for what amounted to the popular inauguration – the excitement and applause of the crowd. I stood with him on the podium in the middle of the Square while the crowd cheered and danced and sang. It was an exciting and overwhelming day, and to see such a vast crowd expressing so uninhibitedly their straighforward pleasure, was a fitting climax to the months of hard campaigning and work. The celebration was a mixture of supporters of the Party, celebrating a victory as in any contest, and the people of Ghana, whatever their allegiances, celebrating a return to normality, and a return to democracy.

I slipped away from the official party and went down to the beach behind Black Star Square; I felt elated, exhausted – and apprehensive. This was the moment we had waited for for many years and this was the moment we had worked for, for many weeks and months. The people in Black Star Square were expressing the feeling that nightmares of military rule and unstable daily life were behind them, and that normality had returned. But were they right? Their jubilation was so undiluted that I wondered whether any future could satisfy them. The expectations of a people are a powerful force, a difficult one to control; no man can direct and master them with precision. We had aroused expectations – could we satisfy them? Any political party is bound to point to the future, and in the present situation of Ghana – or the present situation in Africa as a whole – any political party or any government was almost bound to fail to achieve the future that it pointed to. It was a moment of depression, alone on the beach in Accra, but it passed. For I knew that however many times we disappointed ourselves, we disappointed our followers, we would slowly edge forward and that the future eventually would be ours.

I have attempted in this book to indicate the extent to which we went to try to improve the lot of our people. It is true that some of our people looked at the country's problems with a slumbering air of complacency, though I am sure many others were more committed.

It was obvious that in the Limann administration there were many problems with administrators and bureaucrats who transferred into politics. But I honestly felt that they were learning fast. The unfortunate few who had especially blinkered views on finance worked assiduously to turn the crisis facing the country into catastrophe. But the most powerful permanent theme running throughout the period of the Limann administration was that a weak economy encourages the forces ready to overthrow democracy and undermine the power of the state. The message was, therefore, that we were under an obligation to help strengthen the economy – this must be our top priority.

If we failed in this task, as the coup makers of 31 December 1981 would have us believe, I am sure there is still a recipe for success. Certainly not the Rawlings over-simplified approach to complex questions. We cannot be forced to be fascinated by the activities like those pictures which have the same pictures in them, smaller; and the same picture in that, even smaller; and the same picture in that again, smaller still; and so on. One probably remembers the poetic version of the phenomenon:

'Big fleas have little fleas
Upon their backs to bite 'em;
Little fleas have lesser fleas –
And so on, *ad infinitum.*'

After 31 December 1981, expectations were puffed up and hopes were raised. The public were offered appealing half-truths and Rawlings tried to mislead the most vulnerable into believing there were easy solutions to the country's problems. It was a cruel deception which led to callous attacks on innocent Ghanaians, by mindless thugs. Today, I am sure he knows that the people of Ghana are not as gullible as he thinks. He knows that as far as the economy is concerned, he and his gang have scarcely yet scratched the surface of the problems.

Immediately after the coup d'etat of 31 December 1981, a friend of Ghana was so disappointed that the democratic experiment had failed, he said, 'Kofi, I pity Ghana.' I said, 'Why? Pity is akin to contempt. Ghana is not finished. Don't have pity on us. Some of the greatest victories started with defeat. Wherever God is, there is a Cross.' Though the air is full of paradoxes and there is a scent of decay, Ghana is not finished. We have to do away with the national characteristic which impresses itself on our friends that we are reluctant to make decisions. It is a strange self-doubting tension.

Finally I wear the memories of the nastier moments of life like scar tissue, healed but visible and ugly. I have had my share of nasty moments, but have need them to hone my talents to a full competitive edge – a rough time can make you more determined than ever to make sure you are the best. When you are young you think the world consists of nice people. It is a shock when you turn into a wall of bigotry in a nasty form. But it must make you all determined to win.

With complete sincerity I end with the prayer of St Francis of Assisi, asserting a desire to bring harmony where there had been discord, faith where there had been doubt, and hope where there had been despair.

'Why cannot the good
Benevolent feasible
Final dove descend?
And the wheat be divided?
And the soldiers sent home?
And the barriers torn down?
And the enemies forgiven?
Because the conqueror
Is victim of his own power . . . '

– Stephen Spender